Where is the love?

ANNA WILLIAMSON
CELEBS GO DATING RELATIONSHIP EXPERT

Where is the love?

The honest guide to dating and relationships

GREEN TREE
LONDON • OXFORD • NEW YORK • NEW DELHI • SYDNEY

GREEN TREE
Bloomsbury Publishing Plc
50 Bedford Square, London, WC1B 3DP, UK
29 Earlsfort Terrace, Dublin 2, Ireland

BLOOMSBURY, GREEN TREE and the Green Tree logo are trademarks of Bloomsbury Publishing Plc

First published in Great Britain 2022

A catalogue record for this book is available from the British Library

Library of Congress Cataloguing-in-Publication data has been applied for

ISBN: TPB: 978-1-4729-8672-6; eBook: 978-1-4729-8671-9

2 4 6 8 10 9 7 5 3 1

Typeset in Futura PT Light by Deanta Global Publishing Services, Chennai, India
Printed and bound in Great Britain by CPI Group (UK) Ltd, Croydon, CR0 4YY

CONTENTS

INTRODUCTION

Love. What actually *is* it? I'm curious, what does love mean to *you*?

Do you feel a bit cringe, a bit weird, thinking about romantic love? Does it make you shrink slightly with awkwardness? Perhaps you feel all warm and fuzzy as you conjure up a nice memory or think of someone you adore or who adores you? Maybe you feel sad with longing for a lost love or perhaps you're a bit 'can't be arsed' at present. Good old cheesy, toe-curlingly complicated love – whatever your thoughts on it are, it's fair to assume that we have all experienced love in some form or another.

Love – and more specifically our love lives – are what I focus on in this book. Dating, bunk-ups, marriage, civil partnerships, breakups... and everything in between. Of course, it might not always feel like the L word is taking centre stage in your life. In fact, let's be honest, life is fast-paced, busy and stressful, so love often barely gets a look-in. But it's important. Really important. Why? Because if love is lacking, our relationships will only ever limp along – and who wants anything limp?

As a life coach and dating expert, it never fails to amaze me how often the same issues and challenges come up when I'm working with couples. But the good news is there are some very simple and practical ways to improve the most common relationship and dating problems most of us have.

If you don't have a relationship at the moment and desperately want one, I've got some strategies that will help you get one. If you're already in a relationship, but you've faced up to the fact that it could be better, I've got some advice on how you could improve it. And if your relationship is teetering on the brink, I can help you pull it back. Whether it's how to find love, learning to love yourself, discovering how to rekindle love or – and this is a place anyone can end up in – accepting when the love has gone, we're going to delve into it all.

I'm not saying it's going to be a proverbial bed of roses, but I will be offering you a big dollop of empathy and real talk as I lift the lid on the rules of dating and relationships (spoiler: there are no rules), and help you make your relationships positive, supportive and full of love (oh yes, we're gonna get a bit deep, my friend).

But first, some questions. When I think of love I feel:

a) Pass the sick bucket, you soppy sod
b) A bit of a Lonely Larry
c) Open to it, but wary... very wary...
d) Buzzing with lovehearts, flowers and unicorns

Now dating. When I think of dating I feel:

a) I'm more clueless than fricking Alicia Silverstone
b) Jaded AF and fed up of dick pics – there are no good 'uns left
c) Feeling fresh, fruity and raring to go
d) Don't need dating darl, I'm spliced up already

And finally relationships. When I think of relationships I feel:

a) Rusty as a nail – I wouldn't know where to start
b) Bicker bicker bicker, nag nag nag
c) Passing ships have more interaction that us at the mo
d) Happy-happy in my love bubble

How did you do? If you ticked mostly Ds then congratulations, you're smashing it in the love stakes right now, but don't become complacent. There's plenty more to learn, so do read on to help future-proof what you've got going on. If you were veering towards As, Bs or Cs then fear not my friend – you've come to the right place. By the time you've finished this book I'm hoping you'll be feeling a whole lot better about you and your love life.

We can all learn something – and whether you're smug and loved-up (congratulations!) or disillusioned and miserable, there are things in this book to help you. We'll cover every stage from dating to marriage via bickering and babies, and hear from lots of other people in the same boat as you. I'll explode some myths and tackle the usually taboo topics.

And along the way I'll share dating tips, coping techniques and relationship-saving strategies.

So, let's crack on, shall we? No one said it was going to be easy, but we're going to give it a damn good try. Welcome to your guide to finding (and keeping) lasting love.

1

SINGLE AND READY TO MINGLE

Big breath... OK, let's do this!

Let's start at the beginning, shall we? The gateway to enduring love – and if we're in luck, a jolly good bunk-up – is, of course, the mingling minefield of dating.

I hope this is a chapter you'll only ever have to read once, or perhaps even smugly scoff at and skip over, but let's be honest, even if we're in a relationship right now, we can still find ourselves back at square one again. Whether you're starting out on the journey, or you're just out of a long-term partnership that has sadly run its course, being single and back 'on the shelf' (as my nanna would charmingly label it each time I found myself solo again – cheers Nanna. Where was the #sisterhood there?) can feel daunting, overwhelming and like searching for a needle in a haystack for even the most seasoned dater.

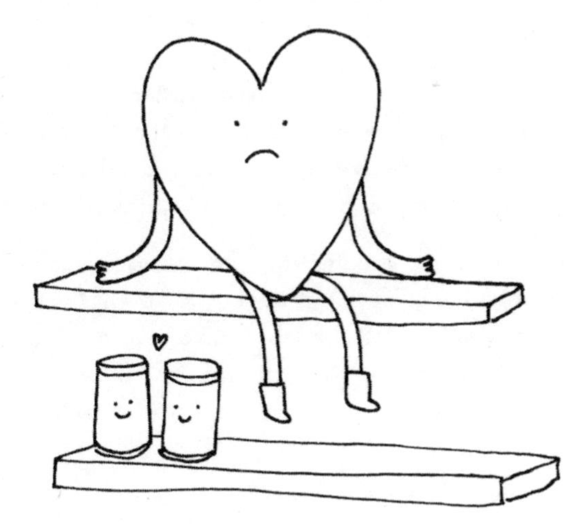

We all want to find 'the one', but let's be real: the course of true love rarely runs smoothly and even if it does, as you already most likely know (and probably why you've picked up this book in the first place), there are many storms that may threaten to rock your love boat along the way. Over the next few chapters I'm going to teach you how to become the captain of yours and hopefully keep it shipshape.

First up, it's all about YOU. Before we even so much as get a *whiff* of a dinner reservation for two, we've got to home in on what's going on with you. We need to shine a spotlight on you and make sure you're giving yourself the best chance to find what you're seeking.

This is me

Knowing yourself, and liking what you're all about, is absolutely key to unlocking the very possibility of finding love and affection. How can we expect to enjoy someone else's company if we're not clued up about who we actually are ourselves?

The most common issue I see with clients who are stuck in the dating merry-go-round is a lack of self-belief, self-esteem, sense of identity and direction.

Love starts within. It sounds like a massive cliché, but honestly, I've yet to be proven wrong. I've seen for myself what happens when someone stops, gives themselves a break, starts being kind to themselves, and recognises and accepts their quirks and qualities.

The bottom line is, if you're expecting someone to be attracted to you, to like (hopefully) most things about you, to want to spend time in your company and treat you like the king or queen you are, then it's crucial that you know who YOU are and what makes you amazingly unique... and a darn good catch! If you're feeling it, they will too.

Finish these sentences:

- My best quality is...
- What I like most about myself is...
- I'm happiest when...
- My greatest achievement is...
- My best friends would describe me as...
- My top three values in life are...
- I could be an amazing partner because...
- I am proud of myself because...

Answer these questions with as much honesty as you can. No one else has to know the answers but you. Read them back, then read them again out loud. Hell, you can even print the answers out and stick them on your bedroom mirror to remind yourself how kick-ass you are! When we see it, we're more likely to believe it.

If you find this task tricky, or even impossible, don't worry. It just means we need to do some more work on your confidence and self-esteem. Don't stress – we're all a work in progress. We're going to be exploring values in this chapter which will help. You can also head to the 'Boundaries' activity on page 46 too.

"I've been out of the dating game for 15 years and I don't know where to start. It all feels very nerve-wracking and different from when I was last in it – eek!"

Dex, 35

Now we're in the right frame of mind, let's move on to *what* you'd like from dating and *who* you might like to meet.

The first rule of dating is it should be fun and enjoyable. You might be thinking, er yeah, thanks *Love Island*, but you might be surprised at just how many daters blindly go through the motions, swiping left and right with as much enthusiasm as doing the weekly Ocado shop. I've lost count of the number of blank, expressionless stares and eye rolls I get when I ask, 'Are you excited about dating?'

Having the right attitude to dating is everything, and the first thing is to get your head in the game and work out *what* you're looking for – and *why*. After all, you're a busy person. You don't want to be sifting through hundreds of booty call invites if what you're after is something a little more meaningful, and equally you don't want to batting off marriage proposals if all you're after is a no-strings-attached shag.

And then the focus moves on to *who* you'd like to meet and *how* to date them. It might sound a bit obvious, but many people enter the dating scene almost on autopilot, with no real idea of what they're doing and what's motivating them – the 100% sure-fire way to NOT succeed. This book is all about becoming more aware and in tune with yourself, so before we start fannying about with dating profile selfies (which are important and we'll certainly get on to those), let's do some vital groundwork and focus in on what you actually want.

I want... does get

There are times when you need to behave like a diva to get what you want. In fact, bolshy self-belief isn't too far off the mark when it comes to you and your dating mindset, because if we focus on what we want and picture ourselves obtaining it, we're much more likely to get it.

- Have a think about someone you like and admire, someone you could see yourself being attracted to (even if hypothetically). Perhaps it's someone you know, maybe it's someone fictional or off the telly.
- Have a think about their qualities. What do you like about them? What attracts you to them? List everything you 'notice' about them as you think about them. Perhaps you could even draw a picture of them.

- Now take a moment to notice how you feel. Make a note of the sensations that thinking about this person, and all their qualities, gives you.
- Next, I want you to close your eyes, take a deep breath, make the vision and the feelings you're experiencing as good as they can be, and make a final mental note of how it's making you feel.
- Well done. You just tuned into what and who you want, and you've given yourself a clear picture and feeling of what that's like and what you're aiming for.

Now, I must clarify that this doesn't mean you should actually slide into Ryan Gosling's DMs (or those of whoever you were picturing) asking for a date; it just serves as a good exercise to gauge what it is you're looking for. When we have a clearer picture of what we're striving to achieve or, in your case, who you'd like to meet, we have a much greater chance of fast-tracking our way to the goal, avoiding the sea of time-wasters and not-my-types in the process.

"I just want someone who's kind, honest, not too short and is looking for an actual relationship, not just a quick shag!"

Sammi, 32

Let's get real(istic)

Whether you're entering the dating scene as fresh as a daisy or you're a seasoned professional, the fundamental principles of dating are the same – intentions, integrity, respect and vulnerability.

You may have never dated before or be into triple figures, but each new dating experience should be treated with the same level of respect, optimism and opportunity as the very first. As hard as it might be, you need to leave any previous baggage at the door, be open-minded and reserve judgement until you've had a chance to get to know each other. After all, you'd expect the same courtesy in return, right?

It might seem as though everyone on Instagram is sickeningly loved-up within about five minutes, but let me tell you, these filtered lovelies are only giving you a snapshot of *what they want you to see*. Sure, there are some (very few!) fortunate people who have one date and –BOOM! – the wedding, kids and picket fence prize package are signed, sealed and delivered in an instant. However, for the vast majority, dating is like one of those irritating PlayStation games (bane of my life): we think we're getting somewhere, we might even be within touching distance of the end level and then – BANG! – game over, back to the beginning.

The reality is that most people's dating history is full of trials and tribulations, ups and downs. Even if it starts with a smooth take-off, who's to say there won't be some turbulence that needs addressing down the line (which is where the rest of this book comes in). It isn't being doom and gloom, it's being realistic – and that is absolutely key to lasting love. I've got news for you, Mr or Mrs Perfect does not exist. It would actually be pretty boring if they did (we'd miss out on make-up sex for one thing!), so being realistic about romance is really super-important. This doesn't mean you have to lower your standards or change your values in any way, but focusing on the 'deal-breakers' of what you're looking for will help to keep you on a realistic path (and in my case able to turn a blind eye to the midnight FIFA PlayStation binges).

Cool intentions

So, we've covered the what and the who, and you're hopefully feeling more empowered, in the zone, ready to take the next step… but what's important is to work out *why* you're dating.

This is really crucial. Have you ever asked yourself, Why am I putting myself out there? What reason do I have to start dating? What am I hoping to find? And why now? It's worth asking yourself these questions more than once, because depending on your situation the answers can change. I get hundreds of messages from men and women looking for 'the one'. They want marriage, kids, the whole works, but I also hear from a lot of people who are done with a 'conventional' relationship and all the trappings, and are instead changing tack and looking for companionship. They value their independence and are quite clear on wanting a 'label-free' relationship with a like-minded other.

And hey, we're not living in the dark ages any more. There are also an increasing number of folk just looking for no-strings-attached sex. They're very much in the market for the physical perks of hooking up, but as far as anything else is concerned, no thank you!

The great thing about the evolved dating world is that there are apps, websites, agencies and groups that cater for every dating whim and desire. Age, gender, faith, sexual preference, lifestyle, financial and professional status – there's a destination only a click away to satisfy that itch, whatever it may be. Once a bit of a joke, online dating is now huge and it's never been easier (or arguably harder, due to the massive choice) to meet people. The key is to work out your intention first – why you want to meet with someone – and then when you're clear on that you can make a beeline for the most appropriate dating destinations.

Save yourself the let-down and dating fatigue by avoiding the wrong platform and take time, care and attention to research the best match for your current 'why'.

Show me the honey

Time to sort the wheat from the chaff, the dickheads from the dick pics. Choosing the right dating platform is key.

To pay or not to pay? That is the question. There are hundreds of dating sites and apps, some of which you have to pay to join, but plenty that are free, although these probably have 'extra' features you can pay for if you choose to, giving you things such as unlimited views or likes of potential matches and messaging options.

There is a school of thought that putting a pay wall on a dating platform attracts more 'serious' daters. However, there are plenty of committed people using the free ones, too. Many people who are actively dating will have a balance of both and sign up to paid ones as well as the freebies, with fairly equal outcomes. The key is to work out YOUR intention so you can sniff out the ones on your wavelength.

Generally speaking, most dating apps and sites cater to a wide range of age ranges, preferences and demographics, and will match you up with your criteria. However, there are also more specific platforms which are targeted to a particular audience.

Here's my top pick of a selection of free apps and websites to get you started. Do ask friends for recommendations too, though, and do your own research before taking the plunge.

Tinder The king of all dating and casual dating/hook-up apps. It's the most widely recognised of all 'meet' markets and offers a bit of everything. I've known people to meet and marry via Tinder; I've also known people sick to the back teeth of the cheeky chancers who flood their profiles.

OK Cupid A dating destination, but also pretty saucy and an upfront sex-positive hook-up app.

Match, Eharmony, Plenty of Fish and Zoosk These are all pretty decent, trusted websites where you put in information about yourself in order to be matched with similar people.

Bumble Hugely popular dating app where women are mainly in control and make the first move by sending messages to any potential matches within a certain time limit, encouraging faster-paced chats.

Hinge The dating app that (according to their slogan) is 'designed to be deleted', i.e. they're confident that you'll find a long-term relationship. Three in four datees go on to a second date with an emphasis on building a lasting connection.

J-Date (Jewish), Christian Mingle, Muslima and AsianD8 Websites and apps for choosing to match with a certain faith, religion or ethnicity.

Grindr A hugely popular app for predominantly gay, bi or bi-curious males.

Pink Cupid, Her and Scissr Popular destinations for LGBTQ+ women.

OurTime and Silver Single Specifically designed with over 50s in mind.

Raya Even celebrities get their own place to play – this is an exclusive (to join you have to be referred by an existing member), celeb-spotting dating and networking platform.

"Online dating for me seemed to consist of dick pics and people wanting to hook up, whereas I was wanting something more meaningful, so I did my research to find the right platform for me."

Lesley, 28

There's something about me

One report from website Maturity Dating suggests that there are over 15 million singles registered for online dating in the UK and 80% of us know someone who has found love online. Research from dating platform Eharmony and Imperial College Business School also forecasts that if current trends continue, more people will meet online than offline by 2035, with over 50% of relationships predicted to start online.

Putting yourself out there, and giving yourself the best possible chance to find what you're looking for can make all the difference, is a seriously good option to consider. If you do choose to go down this route you now need to make sure your profile is an absolute humdinger.

Work it

Dating profiles can be a bit of a pain in the backside. It's hard to blow one's own trumpet, but it's also really important to have a kick-ass, inspiring, alluring, interesting, honest profile. This isn't the time to be a Modest Martha; it's bigging yourself up to the hilt that works here.

Get help: If you struggle to list all your amazing qualities, it can be easier to ask a friend to help you write your profile and select a good image – we can be way too self-critical. If you feel awkward asking a pal to help, write your profile as if you were writing it for someone else so you're not too modest.

Take inspiration: Research other people's profiles for inspiration. Obviously don't just copy someone's bio (that would be weird and catfishing), but looking at what other people say about themselves might help you come up with some good ideas about yourself.

Avoid clichés: Let's be honest, we all 'love to chill with a good glass of vino and a movie' and 'enjoy spending time with friends on holiday'. BORING! Everyone says that, so think of something more original, something that will pique interest and get conversation flowing.

Choose an authentic photo: This is probably the most controversial area, but there's no point selecting a photo of yourself in 2006 looking tanned, toned and... 15 years younger! You'll get found out and that's just embarrassing, and it's not being honest. According to dating app Hinge, which analysed a thousand of its members profile shots at random, photos where you're smiling and/or doing something active (like on a night out or playing a sport) tend to have much better success. Avoid sunglasses and having others in the pic too, because it's distracting and you're not the focal point (which you should be).

Grammar police: You wouldn't litter an important CV or job application with spelling and grammar mistakes, so treat your dating profile and potential match with the same respect and importance.

It just looks lazy and sloppy. And would you select someone lazy and sloppy?

Honesty is everything: Really check yourself and be honest about who you are, what you like (within reason – stick to hobbies and shared interests, not 'tall, blonde and stinking rich' preferences!) and own it! Be positive in your tone (nothing more off putting than a Moaning Myrtle) and put across as much of your genuine, true side as you can. If you love bungee jumping off Niagara Falls then great, but, equally, if you enjoy a walk in nature followed by a game of chess that will be just as appealing to the right person. As long as you own your authenticity, you'll be giving yourself the best possible chance of finding a good love match.

"If I see any more profile pics that shout 'Ooh look at me, I've been travelling', with the clichéd holding a koala/tiger's tail/jumping off a waterfall pic, I'll scream. Guys just need to be more original and less cringe."

Marie Elena, 29

And we're off

Once you've selected the dating platform or platforms you'd like to join, and you've created your dating profile, it's time for the fun to begin.

There are a few things to be aware of once you've opened the can of dating worms. It can be time-consuming to sift through the profiles of potential matches which will land in your dating profile inbox, especially if you match with more than a few. This is why your intention needs to be super-clear before you start, so you can put aside the time-wasters in a click and keep your focus clear to reply to the suitable ones.

Chats: You'll probably get a lot of messages which are simply 'hey'. These tend to be people who are just idly flicking left/right/like without any particular intention. They're hedging their bets that someone will respond and you'll often find a pretty vacuous conversation will ensue.

Perhaps have a quick check of their profile to see if they're worth a response. Otherwise, move on to someone who initiates or responds to a proper conversation and feels a little more invested in wanting to chat.

Safety first: Don't divulge any personal information such as your address or place of work. It's nice to assume everyone is a decent human being, but always err on the side of caution, certainly until you've got to know and trust the person.

Meet in a public place: After a few back and forth messages getting to know your match (you'll determine how long and how well it's going – trust in your gut), you should expect to meet up face to face. A video call is a good next step to break the ice (see below), but at some point you should be open to going on physical dates as most people will be annoyed if you just use them as a glorified pen pal. After all, what's the point in having a dating profile if you're not actually planning on going dating? However, do make sure you choose to meet in a public place and tell someone where you're going.

Utilise video dating: Lots of people get disheartened by the umpteenth turning up at a bar to meet their date, expecting a tall dark handsome athlete, only to be greeted by a short, balding couch potato. It can then be hard not to resent the following hour of making small talk and blowing hard-earned cash on drinks to get through the ordeal, knowing full well it isn't going to go anywhere. Video call dating, which a lot of dating apps have, is a great way to mitigate this and 'try before you buy'. It's cost- and time-effective, and you can do it in the comfort and safety of your own home.

Social media 'spying' is fair game: We live in a world where total privacy is pretty hard to come by, certainly if you have any form of online presence. Most of us have a social media account and with a few clicks of a button our drunk nights out and holiday pics are there for the whole world to gawp at, so just be prepared for cyber space to hold you accountable. Expect your date to look you up in the interests of pre-date research, and there's every chance you'll be 'Insta-stalking' or 'Facebook searching' them, too.

Don't give up: It only takes one person to capture your heart, but you might have to kiss a few frogs to get there. Avoid dating fatigue by checking in on yourself, your intentions, your enthusiasm, and if you need a pause to reenergise and reengage, then do.

“Getting the same guys pinging into your inbox can be a bit annoying, especially when you've swiped left in a big fat 'no thanks', but when you make a connection with someone decent it makes putting in the effort so worthwhile.”

Chelsea, 31

Dating IRL

Online dating isn't for everyone and it should only serve as a route to meeting someone in real life (IRL) anyway. As successful as virtual dating can be, there still comes a time when the online moves offline to face-to-face physical dating. But how do you meet someone out in the world organically? Where do these seemingly rare breeds of 'single and ready to mingle' hang out?

Would like to meet

Have another read of the 'I want... does get' love hack at the beginning of this chapter and set your sights on the kind of person you'd like to meet. Then ask yourself what does this person do and what interests might they have? This should help you expand your options and think creatively about where you might meet your like-minded match.

- Go to a new place each week. We often get stuck in a rut with our day-to-day routine, places we go, people we see. It seems obvious, but try to open up the possibilities of seeing and meeting new people by going somewhere completely new.
- Take your laptop or a book or magazine to a coffee shop and put your phone away so you look more available for conversation should anyone catch your eye.

- Start a new hobby or class, where conversation will naturally be more aligned because you share an interest – it's an instant ice-breaker. Sport, yoga, arts and crafts, singing, dance, walking – find your passion and turn it into a potential dating opportunity.
- Ask friends, colleagues, Facebook, Dr Google etc. for recommendations of any groups or excursions happening which might interest you. Cultural festivals, places of worship, local clubs and venues, and volunteer groups are all potential dating hotspots.

Breaking the ice

Even the most confident of lotharios can stutter and stumble when it comes to asking someone out – everyone fears rejection. But instead of shying away from a potential pie in the face, follow this little checklist before you take that leap of faith and if you do get a 'no thanks' then take confidence from the fact you had the balls to make yourself vulnerable in the first place – and that in my book is only ever a win in life.

Be realistic: Have you set your sights appropriately? Too high? Too low? Is it likely that aloof supermodel will reciprocate your advances or that recently divorced commitment phobe will accept your offer of a date? Check in with yourself before you make your move to get the outcome you hope for.

Spot the signals: Have you managed to have a conversation? Is there a spark between you both? Look for lingering eye contact and open body language (leaning in towards you, smiling and laughing with you). Does the chat flow equally with equal effort and enthusiasm? If so, this could be the green light you're after to ask them out.

Timing is everything: Some people are fast movers, others take their time and let things gradually develop. Don't measure yourself against someone else's pace when it comes to dating. Getting to know someone in your own time is the safest way to gauge if the chemistry is there to ask them out on a date.

Giving you the Vs

As a dating coach, there are two keywords I use with every client without fail: values and vulnerability. Get these two things in your dating toolkit and you're sailing, my friend.

Values

Imagine Superman were to undress you with his razor-sharp vision, right down to your bare bones, and all that's left is what you stand for as a human being. Those are your values. Our values are our foundations, what we believe in, what's important. They're what make us tick and drive our everyday decisions, motivations and satisfaction. What are your values? Examples of values can include:

- Trust
- Creativity
- Honesty
- Communication
- Integrity

- Fairness
- Family
- Friendship
- Health
- Loyalty

Have a think about what your values are and then let your mind wander to a belief you have that's associated with that value. For example, one of my top values (they can keep shifting around the hierarchy depending on what's going on in life and that's OK) is fairness; it's so important to me that everything I do and say is someway linked back to this value. It helps shape my thoughts and decisions. A belief attached to my value of fairness is 'Recognising what's fair in a given situation helps me communicate effectively and reasonably, avoiding conflict.' The belief reinforces the value = unshakable personal foundations.

Other examples of values and associated beliefs are:

- Value: family → belief = my family gives me stability and unconditional love, which helps me feel supported, able to be my true self and confident.
- Value: communication → belief = talking and sharing my feelings with others, and in turn actively listening to them, helps resolve any conflict and establishes strong relationships and self-esteem.
- Value: trust → belief = being open and honest helps me establish trust and transparency with others, building strong relationships along the way.

Why is this important when it comes to dating? When you establish and recognise your values, and then your attached beliefs, you have a clearer vision and understanding of who you are, what you can offer someone else and essentially what you might be attracted to in turn. Someone who has similar or shared values is going to be a much more suitable match than someone whose values conflict with yours. It's not impossible to make a connection with someone who has different values – and of course compromise is always part of a strong relationship – but it makes things harder. It's definitely not something I'd advise as a solid foundation to a relationship.

Vulnerability

This is the second V. Now, before you wince, being vulnerable is not a sign of weakness. It doesn't mean you have to be a wet lettuce and spill your innermost feelings or secrets, sob like a baby or anything like that. Being vulnerable is actually the most empowering and brave thing you can do. It's about dropping any guard, wall or bravado you may have and allowing yourself to be real, to be open, to be the true you. The fear of vulnerability is ultimately the fear of rejection or abandonment, and you'd be forgiven completely if the thought of being vulnerable terrifies you. Most people balk at the idea! It takes trust and communication, and if I'm honest a leap of faith, to allow vulnerability to shine through in any dating or relationship scenario.

Nonetheless, it's important. Why? Showing your vulnerable side stops you wasting time and energy hiding what you think other people shouldn't see, and instead allows you to be your authentic self. Shoe on the other foot, isn't this exactly what you'd want from your other half too?

Being vulnerable is incredibly powerful, but the fear many of us have about it is totally fair enough, because it comes down to control. Being open, authentic and dropping any bullshit façade takes balls. Once you share something about yourself or put yourself 'out there', there's no control over what happens next and how the other person responds. If the reaction is not what you hoped for, it can be anxiety-provoking, embarrassing even, and can make you question yourself. However, and it's a BIG however, we can never change the reaction or response of another person, only the way we choose to interpret it.

Vulnerability is an absolute must for finding true, honest (hopefully lasting) love. It's a risk that needs to be taken in order to give yourself the best possible chance for dating and relationship success. Is it easy? Hell no, but is it worth it? In my experience and expertise it's a big fat 100% worth it, so just take those first steps.

How to be vulnerable

Recognise the purpose of being vulnerable: Ask yourself what does vulnerability personally mean to me? What is your interpretation of it? Can you identify any areas in your life where you can be more vulnerable? For example, have you been hurt in a past relationship and are wary of falling in love again? Can you be a bit cocky or cold to mask your nerves on a date?

Explore your vulnerability: How can I be vulnerable? What do I need to do? How can I communicate best?

Embrace your vulnerability: Change any negative perception you have around being vulnerable. It stands for strength, being emotionally available, relatable and, even if it makes you feel a bit uncomfortable, vulnerability is a form of confidence and self-acceptance.

Gimme some 'tude!

Legendary car manufacturer Henry Ford is responsible for one of my favourite ever quotes: 'Whether you think you can or you think you can't – you're right.' This notion is also massively backed up by one of the main beliefs of neuro-linguistic programming (NLP), which is one of the talking therapies I use when people want to identify and reach their goals. The key to NLP is 'the meaning of your communication is the response you get.'

Have you heard of the law of attraction or the saying 'reap what you sow'? It might sound a bit hocus-pocus to you, but it's quite simple: it's all about your intentions, reasons and motivation for dating, and also your attitude.

The law of attraction

The law of attraction is the belief that the universe creates and provides for you what your thoughts are focused on. It is believed by many to be a universal law by which 'like always attracts like'. The results of positive thoughts are always positive consequences.

If you're anticipating a crap date, then that is exactly what you will get. However, if you reframe your thinking, get your mood and mindset into that Henry Ford 'I can' state and instead project the possibility that it *might just be* a good date, you give yourself the best possible chance of finding a match – or at least having a nice evening, meeting someone new and practising your social skills.

An old colleague of mine was pretty renowned as a serial dater. If she had a pulse chances are he'd dated them. So much time and attention would go into his dating profiles (some were paid-for subscriptions as he was pretty serious about finding a life partner), and, let me tell you, he was a blimmin' good catch too (smart, funny, attractive, own house, disposable income). However, the minute a new date was lined up he'd be backpedalling, looking for reasons why this one probably wouldn't be any good and why it was probably a waste of time anyway. As my dad would say, he walked in the door backwards, ready to leave before he'd even got there! He went into the date *expecting* it to go wrong and – guess what? – it did. Every time.

Now let's take me as another example. To be honest I'm generally a pretty chipper person, but before I got married I'd dated many a fine (and not so fine) chaps. The successful dates which turned into boyfriends (and one absolute corker who's now my husband) were the ones where I'd given myself a talking-to beforehand.

I'd got my head and attitude in the game, I'd left the baggage of the crappy dates in the past where they belonged, and as a result I gave my sparkly fresh new date a clean slate of opportunity to engage and impress.

Now, of course, not every date is going to be a humdinger of a success for reasons that are beyond our control (no chemistry, just not feeling it etc.), but our *attitude* to why we are going on a date and what we want to get out of it are essential to getting off on the right foot. If we take on board ol' Mr Ford's mantra, we really are in charge of our destiny. As my former colleague discovered, if you say you 'can't' then your subconscious mind will follow your instruction to the letter and, quite simply, you won't. But as I (eventually) learned, when you dare to say 'I can' some really rather fabulous things are more likely to happen. Believe me, applying this way of open, positive thinking in a dating scenario can make all the difference between 'still single' and 'happily hitched'.

“My biggest issue when dating is finding someone who would be worth me putting in the time to pursue something with.”

Dan, 32

Reframe your game

Let's give you the best chance to have a great date. According to the Centre of Economics and Business Research, the average date in the UK costs a couple £127 – that's twice as much as it costs our European cousins! With so much at stake, you owe it to each other to get as much bang for your buck as you can, give it 100% and enjoy that soiree.

Before you meet up, just like an athlete would warm up to pull out a personal best, you need to adopt the same kick-ass positive mindset. Ask yourself:

- What am I looking forward to?
- What can I do to ensure we both have a good time?
- What would I like to find out about them?
- How would I like to feel at the end of the date?
- What three interesting things about myself can I share?

Open questions (questions that don't elicit a flat yes/no answer) are a great way to initiate conversation and keep it flowing. Treat the date as a casual fact-finding mission (note the word 'casual' – no army interrogations please!). Arm yourself with how, what and where questions to help you avoid falling down the yes/no rabbit hole. I know they look at bit cringey on the page, and you'll have to make a judgement in the moment about whether they will be well-received or not, but here are a few suggestions to get you thinking:

- How do you normally spend the weekends?
- What's your favourite movie of all time and why?
- If you could live anywhere in the world, where would it be?
- How would your best friend describe you?
- What did you want to be when you grew up?
- If you could invite one person to dinner who would it be?
- Describe your perfect day...?
- Who or what always makes you laugh?
- What do you value most in a friendship?
- If you could time-travel, what period of history would you go to?
- Would you be interested in doing this again some time? (Which could turn out to be the most important question of all.)

> "All the good ones are already taken, but I know that's a defeatist attitude, so I'm going to try again with a different dating app."
>
> Alesha, 24

The dating rules

We've covered the 'what', 'why' and 'who', now it's showtime... it's the 'how'. Dating is all about giving your all and being open-minded. Too many people go into a date with the wrong mindset, expecting it to go tits up before it's even begun, armed with a tick list (ditch this!) or letting nerves get the better of them. Treat each date as though it could be your last. Give it 100%, aim to ENJOY it and, you never know, this one just *might* be 'the one'.

Anyone can learn to be a better dater, so here are my top tips:

Dress appropriately: You're going on a date, so let's give it the respect and effort it deserves. Avoid getting too dolled up, though. There's a fine balance to strike, but wear something 'you'. Think smart/casual Friday night drinks with your close pals or Sunday lunch out-type get-up. Present your *best version* of yourself. Do be mindful of your personal hygiene, smell nice and have fresh breath, and you're good to go. Not only will your date appreciate it, it will also give you more confidence if you're looking a bit dapper. NB: Obviously, if you're going on a particular activity for your date and not the more usual food/drinks, wear whatever is appropriate for that. In other words, don't rock up to crazy golf in six-inch heels.

Be on time: Even better, be a few minutes early. For every minute you're late, your date will be stressing about whether or not they've been stood up. Timekeeping is everything in dating and there's nothing ruder or likely to get a date off on the wrong foot than being horrifically late.

Phones away: You may have spent a lot of time checking and chatting via your device, but your phone has no place on the actual date. Keep it in your bag, coat, anywhere but on the table in front of you, as that will be a distraction and will subconsciously say to your date, 'You don't have my full attention.' If you need to check your phone for any reason (childcare, urgent news etc.), then let your date know why out of courtesy and excuse yourself to check when appropriate.

Be interested, ask questions and listen: Simple as that really. Go on a fact-finding mission to see what your date values. Do their values match yours? Ask them to tell you about their friends and family, their best-ever holiday, their life goals and where they see themselves in five years' time. This will all help you find out more about what they're about. Conversation should be flowing and two-way, like a decent game of tennis, so avoid machine-gun fire questioning and allow your date to reciprocate. Be careful not to ask questions that are *too* personal and best keep exes out of the chat in the early days.

Body language is everything: Be mindful of what your body language is doing, because it speak volumes! Our physiology is subtly brilliant at showing our feelings and intentions. Sitting hunched, slumped, head down, with your arms folded basically says you're not interested and anyone sat opposite you will subconsciously mirror that. Stalemate. Alternatively, sit up, lean in slightly, hands and arms on show/open, make eye contact when you speak and listen to your date. Smile and don't afraid of being (appropriately) tactile with a hand-touch here or a hand on the back there. Read the mood and take your cues from your date on what you feel is appropriate.

Be honest: Don't feel the need to be Mr or Mrs Perfect and gas yourself up to unrealistic heights – no one likes a show-off. Be real, authentic, truthful and open, and if at the end of the date you're feeling it, tell them. You don't need to be coy or play some pointless, time-wasting 'keep them mean' game. But if you're not feeling like it's a date you'd like repeat, also be honest. Thank them for their time and the date, and explain you don't feel there's enough there for a sequel but you wish them all the very best. It might feel awkward, especially if they're a keen bean, but even if they're disappointed, they'll definitely respect you for having the guts to be honest.

The bill: Who picks up the bill? It's an age-old dating conundrum. There is no definitive on this, but my feeling is you should both be *willing* to pay or split the bill. It's certainly polite to offer and shows respect, but if one of you really wants to pay then it's also gracious to accept and perhaps offer to get it next time (there's nothing more awkward or un-sexy than ending a great date with a financial/equality stand-off).

“The first thing he said was, 'How tall was your ex?' Not the best start to a date to mention the ex before even saying hello!”

Megan, 23

The caveats

As with most good things, there can be a flipside. We're all adults, we all (hopefully) know right from wrong and are decent human beings, but dating is a minefield and there are a few things to watch out for.

Catfishing: There are some people out there who pretend to be someone they are not. This is known as catfishing – adopting a fake persona to lure someone in. If someone appears, or sounds, too good to be true, perhaps they are. Ask questions, do your research (try googling them) and *if* you arrange to meet, make sure it's in a public place and let someone you trust know where you're going.

Ghosting: This is such a spineless act and it can feel pretty crap to be on the receiving end. It's when someone suddenly ends a relationship or contact without a reason or explanation, withdrawing all communication. It can leave you feeling confused, hurt and paranoid. If you've been ghosted, tell someone you love and trust so they can support you and help you deal with any feelings you might be experiencing.

Friends with benefits: SO many people have found themselves crossing the line with a pal and moving from a platonic friendship to a sexual relationship. The issue with this type of no-strings-attached arrangement is that unless both parties can remain emotionally detached, it can end in hurt and an imbalance of intentions and feelings. Having a f**k buddy can be a great thing for some people, especially if they don't want the full commitment a relationship brings, but buyer beware: it's not for everybody and both people involved need to be clear on the boundaries for it to be successful.

Bring it all together

In essence, dating is about recognising and deep-rooting your values, working out and embracing who you are. It's about motivation, self-respect, knowing what you want, why you want it and who you'd like to meet. Sprinkle on top a liberal dose of vulnerability and a desire to be curious, and you, my friend, are ready. Go get 'em, tiger!

2

EASING OFF THE L-PLATES

From 'seeing each other' to 'being with each other'

This chapter is probably one of the most important in the book. It will teach you the foundations of a relationship, the nuts and bolts of getting off on the right foot in order to give you as a couple the best possible shot at success. In the same way a child learns the basic life skills of reading and writing, this chapter gives you the fundamental *love* skills that will turn a dalliance into dating.

But when should dating and getting to know someone become some form of exclusive commitment? It's a conundrum that pretty much everyone I know on the dating scene admits is a source of both anticipation and nerves. When, how and who makes the first move...?

So you've been chatting to a guy or girl over text. Maybe you've met up a few times, had a few dinners, a cheeky snog perhaps. You may even be starting to get 'the feels', but what happens next?

There's a rough set of stages a fledgling couple typically goes through to reach the holy grail of social media 'in a relationship' status. It's by no means a foolproof or compulsory plan, and you may skip a stage or two depending on how things are going, but as a spit and sawdust guide the love label ladder goes something like this:

The love label ladder

Chatting or getting to know you: This is the early flutterings of interest, with exchanging messages sliding into DMs. Conversation is flirty and you both put effort into keeping it going back and forth.

Meeting or hooking up: You've moved the messages on to meeting up IRL to get to know each other more. This may/may not result in a bit of impromptu snogging or even 'sexy time'. The dalliance may end at this point, depending on how both parties are feeling (and be careful that your intention from the beginning is super-clear here, so you don't end up feeling used or confused), or it may carry on to the next phase.

Casual dating: This is sometimes referred to as being in a 'situationship' – wanting to be a relationship with someone without committing to being their boyfriend or girlfriend just yet (I know, it can be confusing!). It's assumed you might be also dating other people, which is acceptable as long as you're being honest about it.

Seeing each other: A fledging romance is brewing. You are being intimate in some way, emotionally, physically. This is the start of a potential relationship, and signals are given off to those around you that you're interested in someone and are not actively looking elsewhere.

We're exclusive: Signed, sealed, delivered, I'm yours! Almost. It's not wedding bells (yet), but becoming exclusive is giving a commitment to each other that you are not dating or looking for anyone else.

Making it official: At some point one of you will refer to the other as 'my girlfriend' or 'my boyfriend' and – BOOM – that's it. A relationship has begun.

DTR (defining the relationship)

A while back I had an utterly fabulous, smart, beautiful client (you know the type – they have no idea how much of a great catch they are!) who I would define as a commitment-phobe. She loved the *idea* of having a boyfriend and guys would fall over themselves to take her out and show her a good time, but typically a few months in to dating, just as the guy was getting keen and wanting to move things on from casual to exclusively dating, for no reason at all she'd get her knickers in a right knot and come to me not knowing what to do.

She would say she fancied him and they had a great time, but she just wasn't sure, and it soon became apparent that this lady simply wasn't allowing herself to live in the present, and opening her eyes, ears and heart to who she had in front of her. This is a common mistake in dating.

I used to tell her that the grass isn't always greener, but she was unintentionally hedging her bets waiting for someone else to come along who might be *even* more Mr Perfect. The problem with this mindset is it's risky.

Of course, you should never settle for sub-standard, you should never *settle* for anyone (remember you don't *need* a partner, you'd *like* one – there's big difference), but I always try to keep people in the here and now, to properly evaluate what they've got and where it might be heading if they just gave it a chance.

Bringing my client back into the present and focusing on the potential relationship in play was key to her (eventually) taking that leap of faith with the right guy, and I'm delighted to say they're now happily engaged and living together.

How to know when to go from casual to exclusive

- Your mind wanders to what they might be doing. You're on a work call, you're in the gym, you're taking the bins out... and their face keeps popping into your head.
- The thought of them dating someone *else* makes you feel a bit weird, an anxious chest pang or quite simply jealous AF!
- You check your phone more frequently than you'd care to admit to see if they've messaged and when they do your heart does a little leap of joy. You're also disappointed when a text comes in and it's *not* them.
- You no longer feel comfortable just calling them your 'friend'. Marriage and babies may be way off, but things are definitely out of the 'friend zone'.
- When someone flirts with you, you have zero interest. You want to be with your fledging beau instead of being chatted up by a random.
- You've got mention-itis. Your mates keep ribbing you about the number of times you keep name-dropping your love interest.
- You've also told your family about them. Your folks and your nearest and dearest have heard all about them. This is definitely not just a flash in the pan.
- You're focused and making an effort. Got a spring in your step? Suddenly eating more healthily, popping to the gym after work and taking more care over your appearance? You're full of 'the feels' and feel-good hormones, and your motivation is sky rocketing.
- You want them in all ways, not just for sex. You love their chat, their funny stories and you adore the cuddles.
- You want to know more about their lives, past, present and future, and you're happy to share yours. You're not freaked out by the prospect of 'what if' and 'what's next' for you both, and are happy to have that chat without feeling awkward.

You may not be able to pinpoint exactly when you move into exclusive territory. Not all couples have a specific chat about labelling what they are to each other. It's more likely that you'll agree and confirm that you're not seeing anyone else, and eventually one of you calls the other your boyfriend or girlfriend and that's that.

It's also important to note that some relationships go through this similar process of establishing whether they have the foundations to make things exclusive, but in doing so decide *not* to define their relationship status with a label.

I have a close friend who has been in an exclusive relationship with a woman for over two years now and due to their past situations (both messy divorces) have decided not to conform to everyone else's wishes with a socially acceptable relationship definition. They are instead very proud to NOT have a label. They switch between each other's homes for the majority of the week, have a few nights solo at their own houses to enjoy their own space physically and mentally, and enjoy all the best bits that being in a loving, fun, committed relationship brings. But call them boyfriend and girlfriend and you'll get a stony silence! It's their choice and they're happy with it because they're *both on the same page*.

What works for you, and what you and your partner are comfortable with as your relationship establishes itself, is unique to you and should only ever be your business.

> “There didn't seem a right way to ask, 'Will you be my girlfriend?' We're not 13 in the school playground any more. She just ended up calling me her boyfriend to her workmate one day and that was it.”
>
> Terry, 29

The L bomb

There isn't a handy formula that can tell you how long to date before becoming exclusive. Some couples dive straight in and are coupled up immediately, others like to date casually for a few weeks or months before taking it to the next level. Factors such as distance, personal circumstance and timing can also dictate how long a couple might take to go from dating to 'off the market'.

But once there, what usually kicks in is the heady, hazy honeymoon period. There really isn't anything as intoxicatingly scrumptious and all-consuming as those glorious first few months of being in a fledging relationship. It's all cosy dinners and snuggling up on the sofa. The thought of an argument at this stage – laughable! And then the frolics and fornicating develop even further into oxytocin overload, and with all those slushy happy hormones floating around, one or both of you starts to fall head over heels in... love.

But when should you say it? Should you say it at all? Who should say it first? It's a massive moment when someone utters those Hallmark words 'I love you.' They may slip out in a momentary burst of emotion or their delivery might be orchestrated over a candle-lit dinner, but making that statement of affection and commitment is the holy grail of relationships. Falling in love and saying those magical, affirming words is sweet, sweet nectar. If only we could bottle that moment and have a sip every now and then when the going gets tough, because it will get challenging along the way...

But how do you know you're in love? And how and when do you say it without feeling like a wally and terrified of getting the ultimate pie-in-face response: 'Er, thank you'?

She loves me, she loves me not

One of the hardest things to do when it comes to showing your true feelings is being completely vulnerable (there's a whole section on it in chapter 1 if you need a reminder) and it's perfectly normal to feel scared about revealing this side of yourself.

Vulnerability is about being open and authentic, and taking that leap of faith even when you're unsure of the reaction you might get – that's the scary part. We can never be 100% sure of how such a display of honesty might be received and there's always going to be a risk, but when it comes to love, breaking down those walls and taking the risk to let someone in is a crucial ingredient in the recipe for a true romantic partnership and love.

Vulnerability = strength. It may feel uncomfortable, but it's a sign of confidence and self-acceptance. It shows you're emotionally available, that you're in touch with your feelings and you care. What better way to show you care than by saying those three magical words – but here are some dos and don'ts.

- Do take your time. Too many people confuse love with lust. Don't make the mistake of saying it too soon. It could come across as insincere. Waiting demonstrates that you are sincere and that you have positive intentions.

- Don't get drunk and slur 'I love you sexy-arse' while you're halfway through a kebab on the tail end of a night out. It won't give quite the romantic lasting impression you're after.
- Do think of other ways to say it. Actions can sometimes speak louder than words, especially if you're feeling shy or a bit awkward, so think how you treat your partner. What do you do for them that shows you love them? Maybe you could play a song which conveys your feelings or write a love note?
- Do be yourself. Maybe you're a planner and feel more comfortable working out what you want to say in advance. Or perhaps you're a bit more spontaneous and prefer to go where the mood takes you. Both are right, depending on your personality. Just embrace who you are.
- Don't hold back. If you're feeling it, go for it and say it! Someone has to say it first, so why not you. Embrace the moment, find the courage and do it.
- Do 'read the signals'. Are there any signs from your partner that they might be feeling the same? Is there a palpable sense of giddiness, fizz of excitement when you kiss/chat/say goodnight? Do neither of you want to hang up the phone first? Have you spoken about any future plans together? Listen to what your gut instinct is telling you about any reciprocated feelings.
- Don't be put off if the response you get isn't the one you were hoping for. One of the biggest fears is the other person not saying 'I love you' back and, yes, it can be bloody awkward. But it's better to get an honest reply than a fake people-pleasing one which will only lead to more hurt. Nothing ventured, nothing gained and, if nothing else, you can be proud of your own courage. They might need more time, they might not be as invested in the relationship as you after all, but you'll be respected for your honesty and bravery.

> “Passion is the quickest to develop and the quickest to fade, intimacy develops more slowly and commitment more gradually still.”
>
> Robert Sternberg, 'love' psychologist

The right moment

Some people fall in love faster than their partner, so reading the signs is key when it comes to declaring your love. I've lost count of the number of times a client has said they've made their move after only a handful of dates when it's clear the reciprocated signals just aren't there yet (or ever going to be). When the response they got wasn't the one they'd hoped for, it's taken the wind out of their sails and left them feeling distinctly dejected.

Similarly, I know plenty of people who tune into their partner and their gut instinct, take their time, and when they're 90% certain that it's a two-way affection they drop the love bomb and it's all hearts, flowers and mutual gushing over each other.

I remember the first time my now husband told me he loved me. We'd been casually dating for a good few months. We loved chatting 24/7, either in person or via WhatsApp. We'd engineer moments to see each other outside our 'official' dates (my car broke down one day so I messaged him for help – he was there in a shot!). We were *clearly* very attracted to one another (I'm pleased to report seven years later I still fancy the pants off him!) and the thought of dating anyone else was incomprehensible.

Being half-Sicilian, he wanted to treat me to a 'proper' pizza one evening, so it was in a little, fairly ordinary Italian bistro, with an obscenely massive quattro stagioni and glass of red inconveniently positioned between us, that he held my gaze and uttered those stomach-fluttering words, 'I love you,' It was the most perfect moment and he timed it beautifully. He'd read the signals and was fairly sure at this point he'd get the same response. (He did, because I'd also been feeling and thinking the exact same thing, so he simply got in first.)

In stark contrast, rewind a decade to when I was spending a lot of time with a close male friend. We were both single, lived close to each other, worked at the same company and hung out in our spare time – purely platonically. What I didn't realise was that my usual tactile, complimentary disposition was gradually being misinterpreted for something it wasn't. Unbeknownst to me, *he* was getting romantic signals that were certainly not there (I even think I broke wind in front of him!), while *I* was just enjoying this great friendship.

It was during one of our typical weekly dinners out that he suddenly stopped the banter-led conversation, looked at me all seriously and said, 'Right, I think we both need to stop denying our feelings. I love you and I'm pretty certain you feel the same way about me.' OMG, I wanted the floor to swallow me up! I must have looked like I'd been hit in the face by a shovel such was my stunned silence, which was followed by awkward stuttering and an attempt at damage limitation. Suffice it to say, his kind declaration of affection wasn't reciprocated and after such a cringey moment the friendship never really recovered.

The key to knowing when to say 'I love you' is being realistic, tuning into your partner physically, emotionally and mentally, and seeing if they mirror your physical and verbal affections. Then you need to throw in a big dollop of your own 'sod it' vulnerability when you're pretty sure it's a two-way thing and they're not going to run a mile.

Building boundaries

Boundaries are all about keeping your relationship strong and healthy. They protect your wellbeing, keep you physically and emotionally safe, healthy and happy, and they are guidelines as to how you expect to be treated.

Establishing boundaries is important in all relationships, including with colleagues, bosses, family and friends, but they play a particularly unique and vital role in a relationship to ensure there is respect and fairness in place from the beginning. Effective boundaries are about self-respect and knowing your limits, and that there are consequences if they are crossed.

Imagine a boisterous child, who knows he can run riot and play safely within the confines of a fenced garden (the boundary). But if that fence were to be removed there would be no 'safe zone', no clear limits, no boundary, and the child might come to harm.

In a relationship there are physical and emotional boundaries, and it is equally important to identify them to ensure a healthy, well-functioning partnership. Without wanting to be a passion killer in those early weeks and months of the honeymoon lust-fest, it's important, and useful, to establish your boundaries early doors, so that nothing comes as a surprise or causes confusion down the line.

Examples of physical boundaries include:

- Being touched in a certain way or in a certain place (sexual or otherwise) – you might not be comfortable with your bum being stroked or holding hands
- Sexual exploration – knowing what you like and are prepared to do, and what's a firm 'no way'
- Aggressive behaviour, such as shouting or throwing things in frustration
- Privacy, such as looking through personal possessions like phones, drawers, finances, emails etc.
- Individual time to see your own friends and family, and be alone

Examples of emotional boundaries include:

- Name-calling or using unsavoury language, perhaps in an argument
- Having your wishes accepted without blame or fear of upsetting your partner – if you've said no to something that goes against your values and beliefs, then no means no
- Having your spiritual or cultural beliefs respected
- Owning your own feelings and opinions, and not having them dictated to you
- Owning your vulnerability – choosing to share certain aspects of your life only when you feel comfortable doing so

Identifying your boundaries at the start of a relationship helps create clear lines of communication and a mutual understanding of the expectations you have within the relationship to ensure you feel loved, valued and respected.

Identifying and setting boundaries

Some people find setting boundaries easier than others. Depending on your upbringing, role models and experiences, your ability to understand, identify and set boundaries can vary. Here are a few ways to help get you on the right road:

Check in with yourself: How am I feeling? What's important to me? What do I need to feel safe, comfortable and respected emotionally and physically? Is there anything that might make me feel particularly vulnerable?

Look at past evidence: Perhaps you've been in a relationship or situation before where your boundaries have been crossed? What happened and how did you feel? What have you learned and what would/could you change to ensure that boundary is firmly in place in the future?

Tune into your feelings: How will I know if my boundaries are being tested? What warning signs can help me be aware?

Be kind yet firm: Find a calm moment and don't use threating or angry words of threat or anger. Let your partner know you're doing this out of trust and love for you both, and instead use statements of what you need and expect, such as, 'I'd appreciate being treated with dignity at all times, even if we have a row.'

Lay down the consequences: If you're met with any backlash or feelings of guilt, take yourself out of the situation temporarily to get yourself centred. Take some deep breaths, then quietly reaffirm the importance of your boundary and that a relationship where this isn't upheld or respected is going to be a challenge (and may not be for you).

It's a two-way thing: A relationship is about equal input. Once you've outlined your boundaries, ask your partner to reciprocate with theirs and work together to uphold what's important to you both.

Every relationship is different, but knowing your boundaries and keeping them constant will help start each one on the right foot. I have a hard boundary which I've always upheld – I will not tolerate name-calling, swearing or abusive language in any relationship I have, particularly romantic ones.

It comes from being brought up in a non-confrontational and mild-mannered family, which made me feel secure and loved. Sure, we could all get a bit agitated back in the day, although two annoying brothers and fairly strict parents meant we all learned to tow a respectful line, but it was an absolute no-no if anyone was rude, spiteful or used 'bad' language in an altercation. To this day, I've never had a shouty argument or been disrespectful (verbally or otherwise) to either of my brothers or my parents, so I certainly don't stand for it in an intimate relationship.

Sure, along the way I've had a few 'unsavoury' boyfriends who haven't taken on board my boundaries and there has always been a consequence for stepping over that limit: after a warning, if nothing changes, bye-bye, I've ended it. What you won't stand for may not be a problem for the next person and some people might think that is an extreme reaction, but boundaries are uniquely personal and highly important to *you*.

Don't sweat the small stuff

So far most of the boundary chat has been about some pretty hard lines being set. These are important for our physical, mental and emotional wellbeing, but there are also other boundaries that can come into play the more you get to know each other and learn about each other's little quirks, which, although seemingly harmless, *can* irk and irritate.

I have a client who is in the early phase of a new relationship. A few months in it's going well, they're head over heels in lust and only have eyes for each other, BUT he has a bit of a gripe about her manners and personal habits, which is becoming a bit of an issue. He's a rather private guy who values an air of mystery in a relationship, whereas she is clearly extremely comfortable and 'free' in her disposition (which is a lovely quality), and doesn't mind openly belching (including in public) and cocking a leg to crack out a fart should the urge take her. Now, not for one minute am I being a Judge Judy here – if you need to let one rip, you need to let one rip – but for every action there is a reaction, and the reaction to this behaviour is it's putting him off her.

It's an another otherwise perfect fledgling relationship, but he values manners and etiquette, and he's starting to worry about introducing her to his family and friends. This early warning sign needs to be acknowledged pronto in order to gauge the reaction, have a calm chat about it and agree (if need be) if any firmer boundaries should be put in place. She might not think there's anything wrong with leaving the bathroom door open and having a chat while she's mid-way through her business on the loo. He, however, would rather she didn't.

Addressing a seemingly trivial niggle like this is important, and needs to be dealt with sensitively and respectfully, so as to not offend, upset or appear dictatorial. In my client's case, my advice was to wait for it to happen again and then kindly pull her up on it, explaining why it mattered to him. I suggested giving it the 'shit sandwich' approach – start with a positive comment, then address the irk, then finish positively by reaffirming your feelings.

The conversation went something like this: 'Babe, I find you so attractive and sexy, but when you belch like that I do find it rather unappealing and a bit rude. Manners are really important to me and I don't think it's very polite to burp so obviously in public or in private. I'd be really grateful if you could be a bit more mindful of it and thanks for taking it on board without getting annoyed. I really appreciate it.'

And guess what? She *thanked* him for bringing it up and explained it was an unconscious thing she did, and she had never even thought about how it might be construed by others. It was nipped in the bud before it became a bigger issue and the relationship has carried on growing positively in leaps and bounds ever since.

Your place or mine?

There are no set rules about when you should take the massive step of moving in together or indeed whether you should do this at all. Intentions are what is key here. Many couples move in together as a 'test drive' for the next stage in a committed relationship, but convenience often plays a part in deciding to bunk up together more permanently.

If you're spending more nights at theirs than yours, or vice versa, and you've already wangled your own drawer, taken over the wardrobe and have a toothbrush in the holder, it might be worth having an honest convo with your partner to work out your co-habiting compatibility and future goals. The following checklist might help you decipher whether it's for you or not.

Motivation: What's your motivation for moving in together? Is it physical convenience, because you stay over every night anyway? Or is it emotional, because you can't stop thinking about them and just want to be there for them every day? Spoiler alert: the emotional motivation should take precedence.

The goal: Where are you both heading in the relationship? Does co-habiting have to lead on to marriage and kids? It's OK to have differing intentions about what co-habiting may or may not develop into, but you do need to know what each other's thoughts and feelings are about it.

Your needs: Do you need your own office space? A place to work out? Do you like some solo chill time to play on a computer or take an uninterrupted bath every night? Outline any specific needs you both have, physically and mentally.

Financial communication: It's the least sexy part of a relationship, but we can't shy away from the fact that it's the number one cause of breakups. Rent, bills, debts, income, outgoings... If you're in an intimate relationship then there should be transparency and open communication about finances, and what each of you expect from the other. Getting this nailed and sorted in advance will save you a whole heap of agro – trust me!

Interdependence: An interdependent relationship is highly important. It's when you rely on and compromise with each other while maintaining an autonomous identity at the same time. In short, it's valuing and respecting your individual time as well as your time together, and not compromising your unique identity for the sake of your partner. Trust, honestly and vulnerability help in establishing an interdependent relationship, and if you're going to move in together this is super-important. If you're being made to feel awkward about going out with your friends, or your partner makes you feel guilty in any way for having your own friends, family, hobbies and so on, this is a major red flag (there's more on this in chapter 8).

When rampant turns into routine

Whether you've decided to shack up together or are keeping things as a more chilled 'house-hopping' set-up, there will come a moment when the three-times-a-night shagging and the gut-wrenching butterflies at the mere ping of a text message starts to wane, never mind the effort required to hold in a post-coital fart.

The honeymoon phase is the early part of a relationship when everything seems perfect, carefree and happy. It can last for six months to two years, but it really is different for everyone. The reason this early part of a relationship feels so damn good, and is even addictive for some serial-daters, is that it's new, intense, exciting, and full of exploration and mystery. Endorphins – nature's very own love drugs – are flooding your brain like a love sugar rush, bringing all those wonderful 'I just wanna be close to you' feelings.

It's only natural that these feelings will start to decrease as time goes on. As the relationship evolves, so will you. As the glow starts to fade the *real* you will show up: the one who's swapped sexy jeans for tracky Bs and prefers a cuppa in front of the telly instead of pornstar martinis in an overcrowded bar. At this point the honeymoon phase turns into a bit of a crossroads with choices about what happens next – it's either the beginning of a real relationship or the beginning of the end.

If the only thing keeping you together is the insatiable excitement and newness of the honeymoon period, then it's probably the end of the road. But if your values, beliefs, intentions and goals are aligned, the relationship enters the next stage of romance. It may be slightly less 'I want to rip your pants off every five minutes,' but it's got bags of potential, nonetheless.

More on values and beliefs

To quote the dictionary, values are 'principles or standards of behaviour; one's judgement of what's important in life.' There's a load more about this and some helpful information and activities in chapter 1 on identifying your values and why they're important, not only for your life in general, but for your relationships.

Identifying and communicating your values in the early phases of a relationship are key in its success moving forward. They act as your foundations and a benchmark for your life as a couple. Matching values is great, but if not, then own yours and respect your partner's.

Beliefs work closely alongside values. Where the values are the principles which we live by, our beliefs are the convictions that we generally accept to be true. For example:

- Value: loyalty → belief = cheating is immoral, disrespectful and wrong.

It's a goooaaalll!

Hopefully by this point, things are going pretty well for you and your beau. The boundaries have been set, the emotions have been shared and you're an official couple, but a relationship never stops evolving or being worked on. As life chops and changes, you'll hit bumps in the road and scratch your heads wondering, 'What's next?' This is where setting goals comes in.

Having those honest and open chats about where you're heading, either together or separately, is really important, even now. Couples counselling is often given a raw deal and seen as something negative, as if by needing to see a couples coach or therapist you're in some way failing at that relationship – wrong! The best time to work on your relationship is right at the beginning. Get those goals in place early and you've an exciting future ahead.

My husband and I are big goal-setters, but we review our goals often and, depending on where we are, adjust and re-set them. Goals keep an interdependent relationship not just ticking over (you don't want that – things can start to stagnate), but moving forward with you both actively engaging in being a couple.

Communication – being open and being specific (where appropriate) – is vital when it comes to setting goals. Having these important chats early doors about the big life goals – the whoppers such as: Do you want kids? Marriage? To live abroad? – help in figuring out whether the relationship has longevity or whether some level of compromise needs to come into play. In my experience, both professionally and personally, the kids one is a massive deal-breaker. It's too big a life goal to compromise on if you feel strongly about it either way, so be honest and it will save you both tears down the line.

Seeing is believing

One of the best ways to set goals is to do it visually. Having a visual reference point has been proven to be more effective than just keeping it in your head, meaning you're more likely to stick to it.

You can do it in any way you like – Post-its stuck on the fridge, a note on your phone – but my favourite is to draw or make a future mood board. Do this activity together and make it work for you, depending on what medium feels right. Cutting and sticking isn't everyone's cup of tea so you might prefer a photo board or doodling.

- Take a piece of paper, card, whatever you like, and either draw, paint or make a collage with cut-outs from magazines (retro!), photos etc. of what your life will look like in five years' time.
- Be creative. Think about where you will be living, what will you be doing, hobbies, work, family, pets, holidays, income. Get it all down and really explore all areas of your life as an individual and as a couple to create a picture that's not only aspirational but tangible.
- Stick your mood board in a prominent place. Don't just shove it behind the fridge never to be seen again; pop it somewhere where you'll both see it and refer to it regularly to check in with where you are in relation to the goals.
- Feel free to add or take things away as and when life takes its natural twists and turns, but always communicate any changes and progress with your partner.

Getting the ick

So here I just want to say that sometimes, and you're just not sure how or why, despite all your early excitement and feeling weak at the knees every time they so much as looked in your direction, you suddenly and without explanation get what many call 'the ick'.

It's a dating term that describes the 'cringe' feeling you get when, without warning, you go off someone you've been dating. Getting the ick is more than just going off someone, though. It's a response to something they've either said, done or stand for – something which goes against your value system perhaps, or your particular standards, or maybe their look or smell suddenly doesn't do it for you as once it did.

It doesn't even have to be something they've 'done'. It could be a character trait that you've suddenly started getting irritated by or just some hesitancy you have about not wanting to get any closer to them.

Whatever the cause, the ick is often a gut response and it's not something that you can fake, gloss over or ignore. Should you give them a chance to see if it's something that passes and you can get over? Sure, because that *can* happen, but ultimately you have to trust your instinct and if, despite them being a 'nice person' or 'relationship material', you get the ick then you know that this is not something you can or should pursue.

> “He suddenly went from being the most sexy man alive to making my skin crawl every time he wanted to kiss me. I tried to work through it, but eventually I knew he wasn't the one for me, so I told him it wasn't working for me any more. He was disappointed, but I could tell he appreciated not being strung along.”
>
> Anya, 28

3

FROM BICKER TO BARNEY

The heat is on

Whether you're a few weeks, months or even several years into your relationship, one thing's for certain: there are going to be moments where you feel the not-so-glossy side of love. Conflict, disagreements and differing opinions are par for the course in a relationship, and as much as we can all plaster on a smile through gritted teeth (I call it 'the public face'), when it comes to having a good old ding-dong in private, we all do it. The reassuring news is, it would weird if we didn't!

Anyone who tells you they've never argued with their partner is either bottling things up, because they're not sure how to vent them or lying to you. Most couples counsellors will tell you they are less worried about a couple who bicker occasionally than those who say they never argue at all. A couple who never argue or disagree are quite likely to be hiding their true feelings and emotions, and that never bodes well in the long term.

Let's be honest, few people really enjoy a good yelling match and if you're anything like me, who avoids confrontation like the plague, having an argument is time-consuming, upsetting and utterly exhausting. But contrary to how it might feel (and it can feel pretty crap), having an argument is not actually a bad thing. In fact, in a relationship it serves as an opportunity to confront anything that has caused conflict, get things off your chest and tell your partner how you feel.

Of course, in an *ideal* world when your other half has royally pissed you off, a calm, measured conversation before things escalate into a screaming match would be preferable, but life doesn't really go like that. How many of us can hold our hands up and admit that we've ended up in full screeching harpy mode?

I don't mind admitting that (way) in the past I've literally foamed at the mouth and self-inflicted tinnitus in one of my less 'measured' moments. I'm not proud of it, but I'm also human. I was also a clueless, hormone-filled teenager. I've learned over the years how to communicate better in my relationships so there's less 'harpy' and more 'harmony' when things get heated. This chapter is all about working out why we argue, how we argue and what we can do about it.

Tell me why?

How would you define 'argument'? Some people think it's one person just being difficult, others think it's a form of being uncooperative or awkward. The official definition of an argument is 'an exchange of diverging or opposite views, typically a heated or angry one', which is pretty spot on, but I think an argument can be so much more than that too.

From my work with couples, an argument is also an opportunity to offload feelings, unfairness, or pent-up worry. It's often about self-preservation, exasperation, and upholding certain values and beliefs. Sometimes emotions and frustrations spill over in life, and due to the nature of its closeness, in a relationship, arguments do and will happen.

There are lots of reasons why we argue and there will also be many unique 'bicker-triggers' to your relationship. How many of us wonder if it's only us that row about this or that? Let me reassure you, pretty much everyone has disagreements in relationships and my research and experience tells me they are usually about one or more of these six topics:

- Affection
- Sex
- Money

- Control
- Jealousy
- Housework

I recently did a straw poll on my social media asking what the top reasons for arguing with a partner are and I was overwhelmed by the thousands of responses that came flooding in within minutes (that was indicative in itself!), all saying pretty much the same thing:

- Mess (the state of the house)
- Kids/parenting (feeling it's one-sided)
- Communication (lack of)

It seems we all get antsy about a lot of the same stuff. And a lot of it sounds and feels pretty clichéd, trivial even, but it doesn't make it any less real or exasperating – certainly not when you're banging your head against a brick wall for the umpteenth time after asking for the dirty dishes to be put IN the dishwasher, not BY the damn thing. At the wrong time, on the wrong day, it can be enough to flick the 'f**k you' switch!

Arguments and disagreements can start in a relationship from even a few dates in, but there really is no measure of when or how one might crop up. It's actually less about time and more about when you feel comfortable enough with each other to openly disagree on something. And it's OK – opposing ideas and disagreements will happen in a relationship. After all, it's two separate people, from two different families and two different life experiences. Just because you're attracted to each other, hopefully love and respect each other, and enjoy each other's company, it doesn't mean you have to, or will, think the same way or have the same viewpoints.

In order to work through disagreements, you need to look at how honestly you communicate your needs to each other and how the other responds.

> "The aim of an argument should be progress not victory."
>
> Joseph Joubert, French scholar, moralist and essayist

From zero to a hundred

How many times have you started what seemed like a perfectly normal conversation, only for it to descend into a full-blown barney within seconds – and not quite known how you ended up there?

How do you respond to these situations? Do you have a long fuse or do you explode in an instant? I like to use the analogy that we're like a bucket of water: we can often take a lot, but the closer to the brim we get without emptying some out (sorting out the niggles), the more likely it is to spill over. And it's often a single drop – something trivial like the milk being left out again – that does it. Cue the floodgates!

Everyone has their own 'measure' of how much they can take, and how quickly and easily they get cross. Some people have an enormous bucket, others a thimble. Being in tune with how you react to situations and how you can prevent a tsunami of annoyance overflowing will help keep your conflict communication in a much more helpful place.

Communication is about being both self-aware and aware of the other person. Here's a handy guide to help you know when a mild irritation is about to ramp up into a row – and, crucially, what to do about it.

Level 1 – the niggle: Mildly irritated, eyebrows lifted in a hint of annoyance, trying to keep things cool.

Level 2 – the bicker: Tone and voices raised to a 'firm' volume, a tit for tat exchange has started.

Level 3 – Shouty McShout: Any chance at quiet reasoning off the table, possible pulsating vein in forehead due to the scale of frustration.

Level 4 – the yell: Seriously hacked off, sore throat setting in due to trying to get point across.

Level 5 – the screaming harpy: Wheels officially off, all control and possibility of verbalising anything coherent lost, foaming mouth, possible self-inflicted stress-headache brewing.

I'm of course having a little fun with this (if you can't make light of a chapter all about having a bloody big barney then it's going to be bit of a rough slog for us both), but all jokes aside, most of us can identify with at least the notion of this hierarchy. Recognising where you are on this scale can be useful in knowing when to take a much-needed pause in a heated exchange to ensure you don't reach the most unpleasant (for everyone) level 5.

Levels 1 and 2 are pretty standard day-to-day/week-to-week moments in a relationship and if you can keep disagreements to a simmer and quickly resolve them, excellent. If arguments are hitting levels 4 and 5 regularly, it's definitely time to address what's sparking such a reaction and what you need to do about it. Read on for some tips on how to argue and dos and don'ts.

When arguing can be good

Healthy and happy couples argue. Fact. The main take-home from this chapter I'd love you to hold on to when the going gets tough is that arguing does not necessarily mean your relationship is crap, ill-matched and heading for a one-way ticket to Single Town. Of course, if you and your partner are tearing verbal strips off each other day in day out then you definitely need to address the reasons, but bickering and having disagreements is not only normal, it's helpful in building a robust relationship.

Imagine if you and your other half never had a cross word, never disagreed on anything, never vocalised an alternative viewpoint or encountered hardship. You might be thinking that sounds utterly lovely, but what happens when a few years down the line something happens which tests you as a couple? Life is certainly not *The Sound of Music* with lots of skipping around on grassy hills 24/7 – stuff happens and it's how we've coped with the challenges that have been thrown at us in the past that dictates how well we handle them.

It's important to know how you and your partner deal with times of conflict. From disagreeing over what movie to watch to who forgot to put the bins out, getting to know how you each react and communicate in a tense situation (no matter how seemingly trivial) paves the way to learning more about how each of you copes.

If and when an unexpected crisis occurs down the line, such as a bereavement, illness or a financial issue, you might then be faced with dealing with the crisis *as well as* both of your opposing points of view, which could increase the intensity and severity of the argument even more. It would be a double whammy of 'Oh sh*t, how do I cope with this?!'

Now, before you start deliberately picking fights over abandoned shoes in the hallway and the great loo seat up/down debate, let's be clear: the aim is not to have nit-picking bickers for the sake of it. However, it's useful to notice how each other handles the more trivial day-to-day arguments and then work together to find a resolution quickly and effectively.

I'm going to be frank here: a rather fabulous by-product of a damn good row is the make-up sex. We've all seen the movies when the couple have been going hell for leather yelling at each other, only to then start ripping their clothes off, doing that weird bite-y snogging thing, and getting down and dirty on the kitchen table in a frisson of passion. But it's not just reserved for the Hollywood A-list. Admittedly, it might not be quite so dramatic, but often the more emotionally heated argument is a much-needed release of pent-up tension and frustration, which almost certainly needs to come out!

I have a client who is in a content yet 'fiery' (her word) relationship with her husband, where disagreements can go from zero to a hundred in a heartbeat. They don't do slightly raised voices and prolonged arguments; it's almost always a window-pane-rattling shouting match with demonstrative hand movements to match, which then quickly descends into 'a really hot shag' (again, her words, not mine). Both of them actually seem to thrive on it and they rarely hold a grudge or carry a disagreement over; it's all dealt with in that rather ferociously passionate moment.

I'm not saying this is a perfect style of communicating for you, but it works for them, and the key thing is they feel united in resolving the conflict (the sex helps seal the deal). Sussing out what works for you and your partner, how you both handle the rougher times, and how you sort your issues out as a team will make you stronger each time the going gets tough.

> “I wouldn't bother arguing with her if I didn't love her so much.”
>
> Gavin, 38

When arguing can be bad

There are, of course, times when tempers fray and things can get ugly. It's important to know what your boundaries are and to make them very clear to your partner well before the first whiff of conflict, for when things get heated. What you will and won't tolerate is personal to you, but you should never accept the following:

- Being made to feel worthless
- Name-calling, swearing or threatening language
- Your self-esteem or confidence being knocked
- Feeling unsafe
- Being made to feel bad for your past
- Your partner walking out or 'quitting' as a threat
- Any form of physical violence or intimidation, including throwing things, blocking exits and invading personal space

A healthy argument should feel equal, respectful and safe. It's important to give each other space to vent, offload and articulate both sides of the issue without fearing the consequences.

It's also perfectly normal to feel tearful during or just after a disagreement. This is part of the emotion and stress spilling out, and contrary to those who feel crying is used as way of manipulating an argument, it's often uncontrollable. I'll hold my hand up and admit that I always burst into tears straight after a bicker. I simply can't help it and I have friends who start crying the minute an argument is even brewing! If you're a crier, it's OK, and if your partner isn't one to get visibly emotional it doesn't mean they don't care either. It's simply the way we all handle different situations.

Getting to know you

Identifying how you and your partner communicate in a row is the key to ensuring it's handled healthily. We all have different personalities, backgrounds, triggers, and these unique melting pots of feelings and behaviours all contribute to how an argument might go.

One of my favourite descriptions of 'arguing styles' is the 'protest or withdraw' idea. This follows the notion that we each take either the 'protester' or 'withdrawer' role in an argument, and there are then three possible outcomes. It goes something like this:

Protest or withdraw

Protester traits: Questioning, attacking, accusing, controlling, dictating, blaming, criticising, judging, demanding

Withdrawer traits: Avoiding, defending, silencing, stonewalling, ignoring, using humour, reasoning

Using the definitions for these two conflict styles you can begin to picture how an argument for each of these interactions might play out. Perhaps you can even identify yourself in one of them.

Protest + withdraw: This conflict will typically be one partner having a good vent, raised voice, and vocalising the issue in a big ranty monologue (protester), while the other simply takes the oncoming verbal onslaught in near silence, does their best to avoid entering into the conflict and tries to be anywhere else but in the eye of the storm (withdrawer).

Protest + protest:

Imagine two rutting stags! Both partners are passionately fighting their corner with verbal provocation and stubbornness. Both feel they are right and often these arguments go on and on with no real resolution at the (eventual) end of it.

Withdraw + withdraw:

These two loathe conflict and will, as calmly as possible, state and defend their grievance while being civil and able to reason with the other where possible. The danger of this style is both run the risk of so vehemently avoiding any confrontation that they drop it and simply ignore the issue altogether.

Where do you sit in this model? I'll admit that I've taken all of these positions in my relationship back catalogue, but which one is the better of the three?

You might think that the last one, withdraw + withdraw, is the best as it's less heated, but not necessarily. I've had clients who have fallen into the W+W argument positions and whereas they do get along pretty much most of the time, they really struggle to know how the other truly feels about some things, which ends up biting them on the arse when further conflict arises. Ignoring an issue (withdrawing) is no better or more helpful than angrily questioning it (protesting).

The key is to identify who you are in these arguing styles and who your partner is. Knowledge is power, after all, and once you know what stance you and your partner take in times of conflict, you can identify why arguments go the way they do. Why, perhaps, they flare up quicker than a can of petrol on a bonfire (and last as long!), why you get frustrated when your other half walks out in silence half-way through one of your rants, or why you're one of those couples that never seem to bicker but it doesn't actually make you feel any better.

Understanding how you handle conflict and what you need to feel heard, and the same for your partner, goes a long way to knowing how to manage arguments when they come up. I have a client who is very much the withdrawer in her relationship, and her husband is the protester. An argument would flair up and each would get more and more frustrated and disconnected, due to the different styles of communication. He would need to hammer it out face to face until they reached a resolution; she would need to take 10 minutes away from the conflict to gather her thoughts and work out how best to respond.

As neither of them were identifying the other's communication needs in the argument, it would escalate, name-calling would start and it would drag on and on, with neither feeling respected. UNTIL they cottoned on to the fact that there are different ways of arguing and no one is right or wrong in their approach; it's about working out *how* to meet each other's needs in the heat of the moment.

Once they realised this and had a calm chat about how to approach conflict, they began to manage their arguments so much better – to the point that now they rarely reach the shouting stage.

They've worked out a plan to ensure that when things get heated the needs of both are met.

He asks for a chance to fully offload where she is actively listening and not avoiding him, and she asks for an opportunity to take a short break after he's had his say to gather her thoughts and then to rejoin the discussion with her perspective. They have found this has taken out a lot of the emotional outbursts and frustrations, which used to lead to the unhelpful yelling, and they are able to have a passionate, heated discussion where a resolution is reached in a swift and respectful way.

Break on through to the other side

We've all heard the expression 'putting yourself in someone else's shoes' and it can really help to do just that from an emotional perspective. When we argue or feel strongly about something we naturally present it from our own point of view. We can feel like a victim and as though our opinion is the only one that matters. This isn't helpful when it comes to problem-solving in a relationship or indeed just being able to respect where the other person is coming from.

Instead, try flipping an argument, disagreement or point of view on its head and assume the other person's position. Take it in turns and present the argument from the other person's perspective, switching roles. Really try to imagine what they're attempting to say, what they're getting at, how they're feeling and what the situation is like for them.

You'll find this can help balance out the situation, creating empathy, understanding and perspective. It can take the heat out of an argument and allow a couple to see things from each other's point of view, so they can hopefully come up with a balanced solution.

The dispute detective

Finding out how your other half deals with conflict will really help you in knowing how to manage bust-ups. They will almost certainly have had disagreements in the past – family, friends, exes – so go on a bit of a fact-finding mission to ascertain how they've handled past altercations and build up a picture of how they communicate. Find out the following:

- How and when do they best communicate? Text, phone call, email, face to face, after work, in bed, on a walk?
- Are there any communication styles that are counterproductive for them? For example, do they consider texting time-consuming and open to being misconstrued?
- How have they responded to bickering and arguments in the past?
- How do they usually react and respond to conflict now?
- Do they have a long or short fuse and what typically happens when it goes?
- What's important to them in an argument? Being right or winning, feeling heard, finding a quick resolution...?
- Do they need to thrash it out until it's sorted or do they need space to think?

And now ask yourself the same questions. Share them with your partner too if you feel comfortable doing so.

Once you've found out more about how each other usually behaves in a conflict it's hugely helpful for knowing how you can help or hinder the progress of an argument – you can make a more informed choice about how you react.

How to argue effectively

There are times when we just can't help outbursts, and knowing how to steer them when we're two feet in will help to simmer things down, with hopefully minimal debris created along the way.

We've all been there: a rubbish day at work, a crap night's sleep, a friend who's let you down, stinking PMT... You get home to your significant other and you *know* that you are in a foul mood and should probably not engage in anything that might tip you over the edge, but something happens or is said to push your buttons and you flip. BOOM! A force 8 verbal gale blows in threatening to cause maximum damage.

Fortunately, there are things you can do to pull it back. You may have crossed that line in to Bickers-ville, but you can definitely navigate the row to ensure it doesn't end in a *complete* shit storm.

What

How often do you get into a row over one thing, but then it goes off on a tangent and ends on a completely different theme? Thought so. Often an argument will take place when you're at the end of your tether, most likely you've been getting slowly riled over a period of time. That's why it's so important to confront niggles as and when they happen, to avoid getting to the point where you just can't help letting it aaaallllll spill out.

Niggles are like mosquitos. Unless they're dealt with and swatted the moment they land, they will continue to irritate, hang around and keep biting until you get really f**ked off. It's all about early intervention, and recognising when something is mildly annoying and needs addressing ASAP to halt any further repercussions.

Then there's the full-blown row. The biggest mistake people can make in an argument is flying off the handle due to one thing, which then quickly escalates into a back catalogue of 'Oh and *another* thing...!' This will almost always provoke a defensive response and takes the row into an unfocused free-for-all.

Take a pause (often easier said than done in the heat of the moment), and try to refocus yourselves to the present moment and figure out what you're actually arguing about. Ask yourselves:

- What are we arguing about?
- What happened to cause this argument to start?
- What is the problem we're trying to solve?
- What is the purpose of this argument?
- What's the real issue here?

Often when a real whopper of a barney occurs it's been brewing for a while, circling like vultures flapping around from a distance without actually honing in on the real problem which needs addressing, discussing and solving. So before the slanging match gets out of hand, stop, reassess what it is you're actually all het up about and zero in on that – it's a really effective way of cooling any heated emotions and bringing things back to a more coherent place.

The next thing is *who are you* in the argument? You're no doubt staring blankly at this page thinking what on earth is she going on about? I'm *me*, of course!' But I mean which *role* are you needed to play in the argument? Because depending on what the issue is, working out what your role is in the argument will be hugely valuable in reaching a satisfactory resolution for you both.

We all take on different roles and wear different 'hats' in life depending on what's needed from us and what we need in turn. For example, I'm a broadcaster, mum, wife, colleague, boss, life coach, therapist, friend, daughter, sister... I wear so many hats I should be a milliner! It will be the same for most of you. Each role brings a certain set of skills and expectations. In an argument it's important to think about what hat you're wearing and what role you're needed to play to get a successful outcome. Do you need to be supportive and problem-solve? Are you required to give some honest advice? Are you part of the immediate problem, so need to be in compromise mode? Or do you just need to sit and listen?

Before things get too far in, ask your partner 'What do you need from me right now?' or 'How are we going to resolve this?' They might need support, an open mind, a listening ear, space to talk, advice or counsel, or for you to work with them as a team to resolve an issue. Ensure the conversation follows that route and it will undoubtedly stop it turning into an *Eastenders*-esque screaming match. If the timing isn't right for you to be able to accommodate what's needed, just let them know, and agree to revisit the chat when you're (both) in the right head space.

Lots of people ask if my husband and I ever fall out or get ratty with each other, the assumption being that because I'm a relationship coach on the telly I should be perfect in my own relationship, and therefore we should be like Cinderella and Prince Charming. It doesn't happen frequently, thankfully, but yeah, absolutely. We certainly have our moments when we get the arse ache with each other, but what we've learned over the years is to articulate *what* we need from the other.

Just because I'm trained to help others, it doesn't mean I don't need help and support myself at times, and it also doesn't mean that my husband needs a therapist giving him advice or a lecture every time we have a bicker. Sometimes he just wants his *wife* to be a sounding board to let him offload and work alongside him on a resolution, and vice versa.

Why

I've lost count of the number of friends and clients who've come to me for advice about their relationships, only to admit when pressed on what the issue is that they're actually not sure *why* things are off-kilter. Chances are you've been in this situation, too, where bickering has become more frequent, you generally feel irritated by the mere sight of your other half, and you flare-up at the drop of a hat. And a lot of the time we forget why we even got naffed off in the first place.

Catch yourselves when things are in a relatively calm place and ask *why* you're arguing. Why have things become so heated and why haven't you been able to communicate properly? Bring things back to the here and now, focus on the situation in hand and ask yourselves what the purpose of the conflict actually is? Is there something you're trying to solve? Do you need to say something, but you've been finding it difficult to?

A pal of mine was at loggerheads with her fiancé for weeks. They usually communicate pretty well, but there had been some recent life changes for them both, which turned the occasional bicker into a daily row, and it was really starting to get her down! I asked her why she thought the relationship was having the blip and she replied, 'I just want to feel understood.' It was something so simple, yet so fundamentally key to resolving the conflict – it was about communication.

My advice was to try another way to communicate with her fiancé. Clearly the talking wasn't working at this particular time. The disconnect had set in, hence the arguing was escalating, so knowing that he was usually glued to his work emails she sent him an email explaining how she was feeling, what she needed from him and why she believed they were arguing so much.

Fortunately, it was a good move as he felt a lot calmer reading her honest heartfelt message. After he'd replied with his thoughts and issues on why *he* believed they were not getting on, they were able to reflect, communicate properly, and appreciate what the other was feeling and what needed to happen to move forward. The upshot, once they'd worked out the why, was it became a lot easier to work towards a mutual understanding.

To help you ascertain the why in your argument, answer the following:

- Why are we talking about this?
- Why am I/you reacting like this?
- Why is it important we find a way to communicate without things getting heated?

How

The final tool in your kit is working out how to steer the argument into calmer waters. You've ascertained what you're arguing about and why, but how on earth do you sort it all out?

Language, tone and volume are the golden trio. Get these three nailed and you really can't go far wrong. Most arguments get out of hand because one, or all three, of these components going awry. There is nothing more guaranteed to ramp up a row than using unhelpful (rude, accusatory, blaming, blasphemous, aggressive) bad language, taking the wrong tone (snidey, laughing, sarcastic, insolent) and/or raising your volume.

We all have our own levels of what we find to be acceptable when it comes to language, tone and volume (my Latin husband does love VOLUME!). It's important to check in with your partner to find out what their boundaries are. How do you know when you've crossed the line? And what do you both need to be mindful of to ensure the conflict stays on the right path to resolution and doesn't veer off to an even more hacked off place?

My husband knows that excessive volume is an issue for me and I know that my tone in the past has really riled him. We've worked hard on how we make sure a heated discussion stays civil, and getting these three things right can be make or break.

Language is particularly important when it's comes to keeping things calm. The worst thing you can do when you're in an argument is use confrontational language. It will almost certainly result in your partner giving you THE most defensive proverbial middle finger.

No good ever came of starting a heated conversation with 'you always' or 'you never'. For example, 'You always leave me to do the rubbish jobs around the house' or 'You never give me any affection.' It can be so tempting to mud-fling when we're pissed off, but starting any retort with 'you' will most probably bring out the inner defensive cat-on-attack streak in your partner.

Instead, turn your language and the feeling inwards, put the spotlight on yourself and start such loaded points with 'I' sentences. For example, 'I would love some more help around the house' and 'I really need more affection and would feel really connected to you if I had more hugs.' It's the same issues, but just phrased in a much less 'attacking' way. You'll find your tone and volume will adapt and match the slightly softer language style too – winning!

However your partner responds, whatever they are feeling, listen and validate what they are telling you. The simple response of 'I hear you' or 'I can appreciate how you feel' makes all the difference to feeling respected and, when you feel respected, conflict naturally ebbs away.

To make sure this goes well, you might need uninterrupted space to talk. You might also decide to have a minute of quiet from time to time for your words to settle. To check you're on the path to resolution, ask yourselves these questions:

- How will we know if we're getting somewhere?
- How will we know if/when we've reached a successful solution?
- How will I be feeling when we've resolved things?

Silence is (not) golden: Dos and don'ts in an argument

- Do be honest and say what's on your mind.
- Don't name-call, get snippy or use disrespectful language.
- Do give details – anything that's relevant to the issue in hand.
- Don't say something you can't take back.
- Do be as fair and balanced as you can.
- Don't storm out mid-way through or call things off in anger.
- Do take a deep breath, count to ten and regroup yourself to keep calm.
- Don't give up too quickly.
- Do give each other some space to process what's been said.

Sorry seems to be the hardest word

There comes a point when (hopefully) the argument has run out of steam, the issues and viewpoints have been aired, and a resolution reached. More often than not, if there has been any tetchiness or misunderstanding during the altercation then an apology will be needed.

Why is it that saying sorry literally fills some people with utter dread and defiance? I genuinely know people who would rather shovel manure than apologise. A lot of it comes down to ego, a concern that the apology will be rejected, a defensiveness about admitting wrongdoing and a fear of not being perfect.

For some people admitting they're wrong is a massive challenge for their self-esteem and confidence, and the apology feels somewhat exposing. It's a sense of self-protection and unless you're a complete narcissist, deep down you'll most likely know you should acknowledge any wrongs, and yet you just can't bring yourself to be that vulnerable.

In actual fact, offering a sincere apology for your part in a conflict can be hugely empowering, indicates a sense of empathy and integrity, and demonstrates you're taking a mature responsibility for your words and actions. It also shows respect for your partner – you care enough about their feelings to offer up your own remorse.

Interestingly, those with a stronger sense of their core values find apologising easier than those who don't. Mindfully reconnecting with your own values can really help in recognising the importance of what an apology means. For example, I highly value fairness and communication. I'm also a Christian and believe very strongly in forgiveness. So for me it's important that I uphold my values even when I find myself in a heated situation where I might feel wronged, and when things have calmed down and I can objectively look at the spat from both sides, I will apologise accordingly.

Let it go

The art of giving and accepting an apology is a great skill to have in any relationship. Like any skill taught, practice makes perfect. We might get it a bit wrong along the way, but as long as we keep trying and wanting to improve, we're going in the right direction.

I give these tips to my clients in couples coaching and they've made a huge difference to my own marriage:

- Take some time out and let things cool off. You'll probably not be feeling too sorry in the heat of a row or immediately after, so find some space to calm down, gather your thoughts and think objectively about the situation. Tell your partner if you need space, so they're aware and don't think you've just shut the conversation down, and obviously they may need space too.
- Ask yourself, Is there anything to feel sorry about? What have you got to be sorry about?
- Ask yourself what could you have done differently.
- Ask yourself how important was (or is) the argument.

- Ask yourself, What do I want to gain from this bicker?
- Keep any apology centred on you, how *you* feel and the part you played – it avoids any blame-slinging and any temptation for 'but *you* did this...' to creep in and start the whole thing up again.
- Check your body language and match it to what you're saying for sincerity – eye contact, arms uncrossed and open, body facing towards your partner.
- Put yourself in their shoes to empathise how they might be feeling. It can really help with giving you some context if you're struggling with an apology.
- Graciously receive an apology given to you. Say thank you and accept it unchallenged.
- If you're struggling with a particular situation and apology, suggest you meet halfway to empathise with the other, and to agree where you draw a line where you both feel content.
- Say it with flowers. Or chocolates, or a hug. It's not just words that convey an apology; actions also speak volumes. Identify how your partner best communicates – his or her love language (more about this in chapter 8) – and it will massively help you in knowing how best to demonstrate that you're sorry.

Scream, shout, let it all out

So, arguments can actually be a really cathartic way to get any pent-up frustration out. The art is handling an argument well, allowing each other to have their say (preferably not yelling each other's heads off too much) and coming to a conclusion at the end of it where both of you feel heard.

Communication, or lack of it, is often the cause of arguments, so if you and your partner often find yourselves lashing out at each other verbally, try these ideas to calm the situation before it gets unnecessarily vocal:

- Don't overlap each other. Allow the other one to speak and finish before you chip in with your point. It'll help keep the argument structured and under control.
- Beware of competing to be heard. The louder one shouts, the louder the other is likely to raise their voice to be heard over the top. The result? Complete and utter noise carnage. Mirror and match each other's pace and volume to help bring the tone and any aggression down to a reasonable level.
- Agree to count to ten and take a few minutes away from each other in another room to calm the situation. Make this agreement in times of calm, so you are both on the same page should a row ensue.
- Respect each other's space. Some people need space to cool off, others need to talk it all out straightaway. Notice and respect the way in which your partner communicates during arguments and work out a way to satisfy each other's needs for resolution.

Accepting arguments and conflict is part of a healthy relationship. Don't view it as an altogether bad thing – but DO set argument boundaries and, when all is said and done, take responsibility for your part in an argument. Saying sorry when it's needed will make all the difference to keeping things happy and healthy.

A quick reality check

I think I've shown you that with good active communication and listening it's totally possible to work your way out of a heated altercation safely and contentedly. Hopefully you've also learnt how to argue better, but we need to be real here. There comes a time when, even with all the goodwill in the world, a relationship can hit the skids. If your arguments have become all too frequent, counterproductive and are making you feel miserable, it may be time to accept the relationship has run its course. Deciding on this course of action should never be taken lightly or done on an angry whim. Ending a relationship is full of emotion and consequence, and should be done when both parties feel calm and considered in their approach and resolution.

Couples counselling or therapy is a massive help when it comes to working out if a relationship is salvageable or no longer viable. Either way, having a mediator to help you both offload, understand and accept why the partnership has turned out the way it has is really cathartic in being able to both move forwards, either together or separately. There's more about this in chapter 8.

Do note, though, that if you feel unsafe at any point in your relationship head to the back of the book for contacts for helplines and agencies that can help.

> “He used to throw his phone on the floor in frustration when we argued, which made me feel intimidated. Couples therapy really helped with his anger issues and helped us both feel listened to. Now we communicate so much better and the throwing has stopped.”
>
> Maggie, 40

4

THE CURSE OF THE KIDS

Little darlings and massive dossers

Before I get stuck in with the slightly less fun aspects of having children, I should caveat it all by confirming that kids are a total blessing. I have two and I love them more than words can ever say. However, anyone who ever said having children would bring you closer together as a couple has clearly not spent five minutes in my house at five to six on a Sunday morning after a red wine binge the night before. At that precise moment, all reasoning and selflessness goes promptly out the window, and the minute the little cherubs utter their first pre-dawn chorus of 'Muuuuummmmyyyyy... Daaaaddddyyyyyy' it's all out dog-eat-dog survival mode in the fight to get out of parenting duties and pass them over to the other parent as swiftly as possible.

In my house we call it 'doss mode'. The mere sniff of one us trying to dodge parenting duties with a sudden need to use the loo, an ailment invented on the spur of the moment, or an impromptu life or death email from the boss suddenly requiring immediate attention instantly earns the offender the title of 'dosser'. Our antennae are so tuned into the 'doss detector' that one has to be quite cunning nowadays to get away with any form of lazy parenting in our home. After all, we *both* chose to have children, so it's *both* our jobs to ensure we pull our weight.

My husband and I often muse that we never argued before we had kids, but when we properly think about it that's categorically not true and, thinking back to our 'honeymoon' period pre our sprogs, we're definitely viewing that time through rose-tinted glasses. We can all be guilty of putting those on when the going gets tough.

We certainly didn't bicker then quite as much as we did as when we *first* became parents. My goodness, those first few months and years were a minefield of exploding bombs as we grappled with our new roles – and that's understandable as our lives had changed overnight and neither of us knew what the f**k we were doing. Fear and feeling deskilled will turn the meekest of souls into a wrath-ridden ogre.

Over the years we have learned (and we're still learning!) and we've gradually become more comfortable in our parenting roles. Those initial arguments as we adjusted to having a little person in our lives have definitely eased off as our confidence has grown, but some of the bickers we had pre-children still flare up from time to time. As discussed in chapter 3, our niggles are similar to many I hear from my clients and social media followers, and it can be quite comforting to know that, whether it's the household chores, finances or whose turn it is to cook dinner, we are all in a similar boat.

But this chapter is all about the impact kids have on relationships, for there is undoubtedly a massive shift that happens when children join a couple. Research by Channel Mum suggests that one in five couples break up within the first year of having children and, as sad as that statistic is, I'm not surprised.

Having kids is beautiful in so many ways, but it's a whole new skillset that everyone has to learn individually as well as together, with emotions flying around like tornado debris. Some people take to it like ducks to water, others find it really hard-going. Of course, some relationships already come with children from previous relationships, but however you become a parent (and it's never the children's fault) it can be one hell of a wallop for you both.

Adjusting and adapting to life as parents, as well as placing each other at the top of the tree when it comes to respect, will help future-proof your relationship as well as help you find your way through parenthood.

Ooh baby baby...

Adjusting your relationship to becoming parents pretty much starts from the very beginning and for many of us I really do mean the beginning.

Conception. I'm going to level with you: I don't believe there is anything quite as unsexy as 'conception sex'. I've been there myself, twice, and ringing your other half telling him to 'Get a shift on will you, my discharge is like egg whites and the pee stick says I'm ovulating' doesn't exactly scream wanton sex goddess. When I think of it now actually, I'm pretty impressed my lovely husband managed to 'do the deed' with me lying there like a ragdoll barking instructions at him.

Of course, a lot of couples find themselves expecting without that sort of scheduling and some create a family in other ways, such as IVF, surrogacy, fostering and adoption. I know from many friends how stressful (but phenomenally rewarding) the latter options for having a baby can be, but however it comes about it can certainly be an intense emotional rollercoaster and an enormous test for any relationship.

Taking your relationship to the next stage and becoming parents is huge. Yes, it's lovely, snuggly, beautiful, enriching and all the wonderful things that creating a life absolutely is, but let's not dress it up too much: having a baby is a massive change and strain on even the most robust of couples.

I always go a bit shivery when I hear a client say to me that they and their partner are 'thinking of having a baby to bring them closer together.' It's a massive statement and the intentions behind it are key.

If you're in love, have discussed the pros and cons, the reasons why you want a baby, what that might look like for you both and how prepared you feel for the unknown that's about to be thrown at you, then great. But if that suggestion has come about as a 'clutching at straws' solution to mask any existing issues and as an attempt to force some 'togetherness' or commitment, then I say wooaahhhh horsey – going for a 'band aid' baby is a very dicey decision to make on a whim.

In my experience, professionally and personally, issues which exist before you have kids do not simply go away and get disposed of along with the afterbirth. In fact, they often get magnified along with the emotionally charged role of parenthood. That's not to say it's a definite 'No, it can't work,' but it is important to know what you're dealing with and to discuss objectively all the reasons and feelings behind that decision before you make the leap into Baby-ville.

Baby-proofing your relationship

Whether your pregnancy is a surprise or planned, or perhaps you're struggling to get pregnant or have a child via another means, like adoption, never underestimate how feelings and emotions can swing from one extreme to the other.

There is no right or wrong way to feel, and no blame or shame if you're not feeling as you think you 'ought' to – and that goes for both partners. The prospect of becoming a parent is a relationship game-changer on all levels, and how one person reacts to and embraces the role will be different to the next person. Open, clear communication in the early days of your relationship will help to establish some clear boundaries, desires and intentions when it comes to the 'family' questions.

Only you know how you feel about parenthood, but once you're coupled up it can be make or break to the relationship if you're not singing from the same hymn sheet. Do your due diligence in advance so you both know where you both stand.

At an appropriate time (i.e. when you're not stressed), openly and honestly communicate the following:

- How do you each feel about having children?
- Is there a time line/ideal time mapped out for when you'd like children?
- How important is it to you to have/create a child/family?
- Is having/not having children a deal-breaker? Why?
- How would you feel if either of you couldn't have children? Would you be open to other options?
- Is there anything important you feel your partner should know about you and the 'parenting' topic?
- Do you have any fears around conceiving, pregnancy, birth or parenting?
- Have you thought about what kind of a parent you'd be? Describe anything that's important to you, i.e. cultural upbringing, discipline, parenting style...

All these questions might feel a bit heavy, unnecessary even, at first glance. However, I've had so many clients call me up saying they're having relationship issues and when I've probed it centres around opposing ideals about children and parenting. It might not be a particularly easy conversation, but it's enlightening and absolutely fundamental in those early dating days to establish joint relationship goals, even if the answers aren't the ones you're hoping for.

It at least gives you a clear picture to make a decision on the future of the relationship. Trust me, it's better to know before there's a bubba in the oven, or you're six months into an adoption application, than to discover any misaligned intentions when it's too late.

A friend of mine knows only too well the importance of the 'baby' conversation. She'd been with her partner for five years and had always made it clear to him that she hoped to have a baby one day. He already had a teenage son from a previous relationship and, unbeknown to her, didn't want any more. They never had 'the chat' and, as in love as they were, he'd coasted along hoping she'd never really want to action the baby idea. As each year passed, she got her hopes up more and more about when they might try for a baby.

It all came to a head when she eventually issued an ultimatum and he rejected it. Neither one was right or wrong for wanting/not wanting children. It's too massive a decision to make if your heart's not in it, but suffice to say the relationship sadly ended as the 'goal' was not aligned. Had they had an honest, open chat much earlier on, they would have perhaps saved themselves a very painful breakup or not have got together in the first place.

My own experience of having this conversation is that it actually sped up my marriage and revealed some very important opinions around having children. My husband and I had only been dating for a few months when, over dinner one night, one of us (probably me) brought up the topic of having kids. Knowing how much of deal-breaker this was for me (I'd wanted children for yonks) I was completely open and honest about my desire for a family, possibly even three sproggos if I was lucky enough. My husband (then my very new boyfriend) confidently explained how having a family was one of his top priorities and even though at the time he was 'only' in his mid-20s (and seven years younger than me) it was something he really wanted too, and sooner rather than later.

Well, ding ding ding! Jackpot! In that one conversation our values and life goals fitted together like a beautiful jigsaw puzzle. Our shared desire for a family – and not one that was just a pinprick vision in the distance – sealed our deal. We got engaged three months later and were expecting our first child within the year.

Whatever your thoughts are about having kids, always be honest about your feelings from the beginning, particularly if you have a strong opinion or it could be a deal-breaker. It's OK to want them, it's OK not to, it's OK not to know yet, and it's OK if you have an issue or concerns which might pose a challenge on becoming a parent. The important thing is to embrace that vulnerability and truth, and communicate it to the one person who needs to know – your partner. In mine, and many of my friends' and clients' experience, it saves a lot of problems in the future.

> "I wanted a baby for years, but when I got pregnant, I was so anxious about giving birth that I struggled to enjoy it. My husband couldn't understand why I was so moody and tearful. He was full of joy and frustrated that I couldn't always share in his excitement. It was a challenging time and not exactly the fun and loving experience we'd assumed it would be."
>
> Katie, 38

Expecting the unexpected

There's a great book called *You're Pregnant Too, Mate!*, which I found my husband tucked up in bed one night reading when I was expecting our firstborn. It's by Gavin Rodgers and it's such a good title, because it completely sums up how expectant fathers and birth partners often feel while dealing with the wrath of their preggers missus – *dragged* along cluelessly for the nine-month ride.

In my coaching practice I hear a lot from couples who report first encountering issues in their relationship during pregnancy. 'But it should be such a magical time,' I hear. 'I didn't realise she'd be so moody' and 'He was so unsympathetic' others will say. It's often the first major thing a couple has gone through where it affects both parties equally (in terms of being expectant parents).

If you've 'done it the traditional way,' as my mother would put it, and got married first, then you may have had a bit of a run-up to gauge how each of you copes in stressful situations. I know my own engagement and marriage was a massive 'tell all' for how my husband and I handled relationship milestones – who knew he was a massive groom-zilla? But, actually, the fact my husband wanted to be so proactive in the planning of table favours and bridesmaids' gifts gave me a really valuable insight into how much of a hands-on dad he might be in the future.

And I was right. He's a terrific father. However, by his own admission he wasn't quite the sympathetic micromanaging supportive baby-daddy he could have been when I was expecting our son. If I'm being fair to him, though, neither of us knew what pregnancy was going to be like.

Like many couples, we had reached a point in our relationship where we'd committed to each other and excitedly felt the next step was to start a family. The prospect of trying for a baby and seeing what might happen was equally thrilling and nerve-wracking. As it turned out, we were one of the lucky ones. I fell pregnant pretty quickly and although we were both exhilarated, we were clearly terrified! Neither of us had a clue what to expect (no one does), and I certainly underestimated what a slog for the mind and body carrying a little one can be.

My husband couldn't for the life of him relate to how I was feeling and those nine months were a whirlwind of not only trying to fathom out the baby bombshell that was about to hatch out of my vagina, but also working out how our relationship was going to evolve so we both felt happy and supported.

Communicate clearly and educate yourselves is the best advice I could ever give. If you don't understand something, ask the question and find the answer. My husband thought my sudden overnight 'meat aversion' and yelling at him to become a vegetarian was highly irrational, but he couldn't possibly relate to morning sickness (I actually had evening sickness) and how even a whiff of a dreaded trigger food (steak) could render me a retching, angry, tearful mess.

Then there are the hormones (they really are a bitch), the fluid retention, fluctuating sex drive, fears over the upcoming scans, birth decisions, confidence... the list goes on. It's important to recognise that you *both* play an important part in the carrying, caring and raising of your offspring, so working together as a team from pregnancy through to birth is so important. Too many birth partners feel left out or left behind in the planning of it all, and too many expectant mums feel they are trying to cope physically and mentally solo when they have a partner who could help share the load, if not physically, then mentally and emotionally.

Preparing for a baby is undoubtedly an exciting time, but it's also a massive test of a relationship and one that shouldn't be underestimated or brushed under a carpet labelled 'hormones'. It's perfectly natural and extremely common for both parents to have a wobble, cry or freak out at some point along the way. Support each other, talk to each other and listen to each other. You're in this together and as long as you've got each other, you're going to be peachy.

We've got this – couple goals!

Some couples find pregnancy a really loving, bonding time and others find it can drive a wedge into what used to be a solid couple. However you feel, sharing with your partner any thoughts, ideas, fears, concerns and questions as it ramps up to the birth day will help keep your relationship on the same page and united as a team. Create a shared 'couple goal' and write it down as a positive statement. For instance:

- We look forward to growing and nurturing our healthy and happy family.
- We promise to make quality time for each other.
- Together, as a team, we're going to get everything ready for the baby.

Once you have your shared goal, stick it somewhere visible, such as the fridge, and keep it in mind as you go about your day-to-day business. Check in together each week to see where you are in relation to the goal. Call a 'couple summit' and, with the goal in mind, ask yourselves questions such as:

- Is there anything I need to communicate to my partner to help keep the goal on track?
- What needs to happen to reach the goal?
- What can I do to help my partner reach the goal?
- What do I need from my partner?
- How much do I want to achieve the goal?
- What will it be like when we've reached the goal?

Setting couple goals, having a vision or mood board (we created one of these in chapter 2) and regularly checking in on how the shared effort towards the goal is going will help keep things on track, and moving forward towards that shared vision.

Teamwork makes the dream work

Someone once asked me what being a mum has taught me. I summed it up in three words: patience, compromise and communication. Obviously being 'mama' has also taught me what it's like to have unconditional heart-bursting love which oozes from me by the bucketload for my little sproglets, but there's been nothing quite as impactful on my life and relationship than having children – the good and, shall we say, the more *challenging* aspects.

And I know I'm not alone. Many people tell me that they've never had to work on their communication skills and self-regulate their emotions quite as much as when they're juggling a family. I find my coaching help is in particular demand when a client couple has recently had a little one. They're typically a year or so in and just as they're getting the hang of the parenting malarkey, and perhaps a little bit more sleep under their belts, it's like there's an awakening through the fog and the spotlight turns inwards. Suddenly they're evaluating their relationship and picking holes where it feels unbalanced or 'in trouble'. The danger when a couple has children is that they're at risk of neglecting the one thing that helped make their little cherub in the first place – each other.

Now I know this can feel phenomenally difficult when you're grappling with nappies and broken nights, but this is why it's important to keep the focus on your relationship throughout those early baby stages, right through into toddlerhood and beyond. As hard as it can be with the distraction of a baby, you need each other and your relationship needs you. Many parents are guilty of gradually shoving each other down the pecking order of priorities once a little person takes over the household, but it's never been more important to stick together and support each other's needs. If not, this is where the dreaded relationship resentment can kick in and, if left undealt with, it can grow from a crack into a canyon.

If left to fester, that chasm can grow and grow over the years with gripes, habits and learned behaviour burrowing their roots further and deeper into your relationship and family life, threatening to sap the love and laughter out of your once happy-go-lucky duo.

While researching this book, I asked several parent friends (mainly women, but some chaps too) with different aged kids to share with me the issues and challenges which they felt caused the most friction in their relationships. Without much probing the floodgates opened! These three came up again and again:

- Mess
- Rules and discipline
- Dividing of the chores

'I'm sick of the constant mess,' 'My husband never backs me up with the kids' and 'I do everything!' were just some of the exasperated responses I got. And these were from couples who considered themselves to be pretty happy!

The overwhelming common denominator amongst these issues is communication. It seems most of us have gripes around these topics and I lost count of similar messages that were literally flying into my inbox – people clearly *needed* to vent! I heard about everything from the constant shit-tip the house was in, shoe-strewn doorways, pants dumped anywhere but *in* washing baskets, and breakfast dishes still waiting to be cleared by the 'magical cleaning fairy' at nightfall to backing each other up when setting and enforcing rules, and making another sodding World Book Day costume.

When I asked couples to break down what they felt was the cause of this day-to-day (low level) conflict, they all reported poor communication and in a lot of cases an 'assumption'. You may have heard the saying, 'Assumption is the mother of all f**k-ups,' and when it comes to relationships and communication, I have to agree: 'Oh but I just assumed she preferred to do XYZ...' and 'I didn't realise he'd like to be more involved...'

Couples genuinely seem shocked and surprised when I encourage them to talk to each other about their seemingly 'silly' niggles. When they realise they've been plodding along pissed off in a whole world of poorly made assumptions, you see the mist start to clear between them as they begin to communicate properly.

Often the real issue is what the assumption represents, as one of my couple client interactions demonstrates:

The issue

Her: 'I'm tired of being the only one who sorts the kids' mealtimes out.'

Him: 'I'm a bit embarrassed to cook as I've no idea what the kids should eat.'

The assumption

Her: 'He's a lazy sod and leaves it all to me.'

Him: 'She loves cooking and is much better at it than me.'

The problem with this seemingly trivial issue, which was actually causing major snippy-ness at mealtimes, is that neither him nor her were communicating properly or working as a team! She felt that the task of feeding their kids was falling solely on her shoulders, and he was sick of being criticised for his cooking, so was reluctant to even suggest giving it a go.

After some much-needed time out to talk over their issues, they realised how separate they'd become in their parenting techniques. Mealtimes were a massive bug bear, it turned out. Having permanently hungry, growing children was a massive change from the pre-kid days of just bunging some bread in the toaster whenever they felt a bit peckish. Deep down she wanted nothing more than for him to offer to help out and share the load, which would give her some respite from the daily responsibility, and he was quite keen to discover his inner Jamie Oliver.

The solution: they both *communicated* what they'd like to do and why it was important, they *compromised* on who was going to do what and when, and they demonstrated *patience* with each other to allow the task to be carried out successfully. He learnt how to cook some family favourites and she gave him the space and appreciation to do so. I'm delighted to report that now when it comes to family mealtimes they have a fab system in place where she does a few weeknights, he does a few too, and at the weekend they all enjoy a takeaway. The perfect execution of my PCC rule – patience, compromise and communication = happy mum and dad (and well-fed children to boot).

There are, of course, times when this type of exchange isn't quite so straightforward – the jigsaw puzzle pieces that slot together with some effective communication are perhaps not even there in the first place. It's one thing assuming wrongly or being misunderstood, it's another thing not noticing the issue in the first place. For example, standards of mess is a massive bone of contention in a lot of couples and households; what one person deems untidy, is another person's pristine palace. Some people really care about tidiness, and others really don't see what the fuss is about.

This, my friend, is where we have to be clear, concise and up front about what's important to you, what you feel needs to be done, and when/how/who. There's no point quietly seething away as you feel you're the only one carrying the can, and it's not about handing down a shopping list of demands, because you're likely to be met with a stony face. It's about communicating what you value and why it's a big deal for you.

Rarely do two people *completely* align when it comes to family living. You might like the washing up done the instant dinner is over; he might prefer to leave it until the morning (or not even notice it needs doing at all!). Just because one of you has certain standards, it doesn't mean it's right or should dictate the relationship, BUT it should be discussed, recognised and, where possible, a compromise should be found.

Good cop, bad cop

If you're after perfect harmony in not only your relationship, but your home too, you need to work together as a team. Kids are clever little buggers and are seemingly programmed to play their folks off against each other from the moment they're able to flutter their little eyelashes. And it doesn't stop as they emerge from toddlerhood, so you've got to have your wits about you right through to the teenage years.

There are many times when I've seen the bad cop/good cop parenting style cause massive resentment and discord among an otherwise loving couple, so unless you're a united front, it's going to get stormy. For example, it's not fair for one parent to be the 'rule enforcer' and the other to be a 'soft touch', giving in and undermining the other parent, undoubtedly causing a divide in affections.

Our children know that it's pointless sneaking off to the other parent for the answer they're hoping for – usually in response to 'Can I have a sweet?' – because my husband and I have demonstrated from day one that Mummy and Daddy are a team and what the other says, goes.

We're like a tight rugby scrum. Whatever the situation or decision, there is never any break in the chain, certainly not in front of the pleading/whinging faces looking up at us. They learnt pretty quickly not to bother asking the other and when it comes to the kids, we speak and act as one (almost all the time anyway!).

Establishing your parenting styles, your values, your ideals and your boundaries are going to help in creating an unbreakable team. It might sound a little harsh, but as a couple it's often you against the little, and the not so little, ones!

Take some time to work out what's important to you both and draw up a parenting plan to ensure you're both on the same page when it comes to the kids. This will need to be reviewed and tweaked several times along the way as they evolve from tantruming toddlers to testy teens.

What areas need clear boundaries set? Children's bedtimes, nutrition, tech time, personal belongings, respectful language and behaviour, and chores are some of the most common.

And what do you feel is an appropriate way to discipline as a consequence for crossing the boundaries? Whether your style is removing privileges, banning tech time, using the 'time out' step (for younger ones) or having a discussion, work out what you both feel comfortable with in terms of establishing discipline. Communicate this to the whole family in an age-appropriate way and be consistent in upholding it.

When you work as a team, you're more likely to feel happier, more confident and more satisfied with your parenting, relationship and family life. Children also feel more secure and learn respectful communication. They might be thoroughly fed up at the time, but let me tell you from the hundreds of kids I've counselled, they need and actually crave boundaries. Not having a boundary to push against and test is an overwhelming wilderness.

The parenting plan

Time to unite Team Parent and create the framework for working together. Discuss and clarify the following to create your parenting plan. I've given you a few ideas to help get you started:

- What kind of a parent are you? A strict one, a 'routine' one, an easy-going one, a disciplinarian?
- What are your thoughts on boundaries? How important are they? What are your boundaries?
- What rules did your family have when you were growing up? Were they around strict bedtimes, eating habits, discipline, something else?
- What happened if you went against the rules or were naughty? Were you grounded, smacked, told off or was there no response?
- What do you think is fair or unfair discipline? This is the controversial smacking debate!
- What boundaries do you want to set for your children? You might want to think about respectful language and behaviour, chores, bedtimes and so on.
- How will these rules be upheld? Family talks? Reward charts? Punishments?
- Is there anything you find uncomfortable or difficult about establishing boundaries and holding firm with the consequences of breaking them? Maybe this is due to your own childhood, your past experiences, a lack of confidence or perhaps you're just unsure how to do it?
- How do you feel about possibly having to be 'bad cop' sometimes? Is it a concern or maybe you consider it unfair? Or perhaps you'll find it easy to take on that role?
- What is important for you when it comes to working together as a team on this? To be listened to, respected, supported...?
- What will it be like if you don't set some ground rules as a parent team? Will you feel disrespected, frustrated, disconnected from each other or could it create confidence issues?

"My wife usually sets the rules with the kids' bedtimes and I have to back her up otherwise all hell breaks loose!"

Mark, 36

Sleep! Glorious sleep!

There is nothing that becomes more of an obsession than getting enough sleep. It's hands down the number one gripe, groan and top of the wish list for every parent I know. Sleep is responsible for a hell of a lot when it comes to feeling mentally and physically well, and I am an enormous advocate of getting enough of it.

There's a reason why sleep deprivation is universally recognised as one of the cruellest forms of torture. It breaks the mind and the spirit, and when there are slim pickings it certainly impacts your family and relationship.

We all joke about kids being 'sleep thieves' and surviving on a caffeine IV drip to get through the day, but behind closed doors the impact of lack of sleep can be catastrophic. One of the first things I recommend to parent couples who are seeking help for their fractured relationship is to get some decent sleep under their belt before they attempt anything else to repair it. You can't focus on anything properly if you can't think straight due to sleep deprivation.

Being knackered isn't going to have you skipping around like a spring lamb; it's going to make you feel irritable, emotional and short-tempered. Kids, God bless them, seem not to need sleep when you need it the most. Most parents I know with smaller kids are up at the crack of a sparrow's fart and some of the desperate pre-6am bartering I've heard so that they can bagsy not getting up with them is quite astonishing.

The promise of sexual favours, breakfast in bed, a free pass/mates' night out, back massages, a day off childcare… I've heard it all and all for an extra 20 minutes in bed at some ungodly hour! It seems that in that moment of sleepy desperation we are willing to offer up anything to our partner *if only* they'd look after the kids (instead of you) to give you a bit more shut eye.

I'll admit it myself, I've vowed to give my husband the world in exchange for him taking over an early morning of CBeebies and Lego building with our two. In the moment you will literally agree to anything (you just secretly hope they'll forget about cashing in the promise).

And then there's the competitive tiredness. If you haven't got into the bartering for time to sleep, there will most certainly be a phase of resenting your other half for daring to sleep when you can't. I remember only too well staring at my snoozing husband as I desperately tried to latch our newborn onto my swollen boob, secretly wanting to wallop his smug sleeping face – how dare he!

In some of our less fine moments we've tried to get one up on the other by trying to figure out who's had 15 minutes more sleep than the other. It sounds utterly ridiculous when I write it down, but in the moment, when you're battling the permanent feeling of jetlag and desperate for a someone to take over your responsibilities so you can get some more sleep, it feels the most important thing ever.

The best advice I was given around parenting and sleep was never to chase it. You'll never win that battle and it'll likely send you round the bend with the never-ending obsession of trying to make up for lost ZZZs. The more you stress about it, the less you'll be able to drop off when an opportunity arises. Acceptance can be hugely powerful, so instead of desperately craving more and planning your entire life around it, allow yourself to just relax, go with the flow, and when and if you can have an impromptu kip (I used to find in the car, parked up, when the kids had fallen asleep on the way home from Tesco a godsend for forty winks), go for it.

How to sleep easy

Everyone seems to have little tips, techniques and hacks to maximise the minimal sleep you often get as a parent. These are some of my favourites.

It's not for ever: In the early days, when your baby is a newborn, prepare mentally for feeling 'jetlagged' and having broken nights. It feels crap, but it doesn't last – it's important to remember that at 2am on the milk merry-go-round.

Put a sleep system in place: My husband and I did 'shifts' in the early weeks and months. I would go to bed at 8pm and sleep uninterrupted until the 3am feed, and he would stay up, do the 11pm feed and then sleep through until morning when he could go to work feeling fairly rested. It was a massive change from hanging out together drinking wine and watching crap on the TV, but it was necessary for our mental health and for our relationship. We worked as a team and it worked for us. If you're exclusively breastfeeding this might not work for obvious reasons (you'll be in demand!), but you might consider expressing into a bottle if you'd like to try this option (that's what we did).

Ask for help: A parent, family member, friend, sleep nanny – don't be too proud if you feel like you need some help... and some sleep. I have a friend whose mum would come round every Saturday night to do the night feeds while she and her husband enjoyed a full night's sleep together. It made getting through the week easier and reduced tiredness-infused bickering as they knew they had that to look forward to.

Get your bed back: Does 'There were three in the bed and the little one said roll over...' sound familiar? As much as we all love our children, we do not like them so much at 3am when they've highjacked our bed and are sprawled out like a starfish, booting us both in the ribs. Passion and sleep killer – yes. Research sleep training with your little one. Treat it as an important thing to crack and work as a team to reclaim your privacy, couple time in bed and sleep.

Take turns: There will be days when you're feeling rubbish. Maybe you've got a hangover (there is nothing more painful than looking after the kids when you've got a hangover – fact!) or just need a bit of TLC. Compromise with your partner and 'take one for the team' to get some restorative sleep in. Both of you tired is a recipe for a row, so take turns being the on-duty parent to let the other have a rest. Everyone benefits.

Engineer a break: If and when it's possible, ask someone you trust to look after the little one(s) for a night or two so you can have some respite. A hotel, a B&B, even just staying at home if the kids can stay over with their grandparents will help you to reconnect with each other, have a much-needed uninterrupted lie-in and, you never know, with no little people around to burst in maybe even some nooky!

Rules to reduce worrying: It's not just the little ones. Teenagers can be responsible for their parents' sleepless nights for completely different reasons! Worrying about where they are, who they're with, if they're safe... Just when you think you can finally enjoy a lie-in, you find yourself up half the night worrying sick about the whereabouts of your wayward teen. Keep open, non-judgemental communication as a high priority with your older kids. If they know you care but also trust and respect them, they're more likely to respect you and your wishes in turn. Set rules on tech time, coming home times and letting you know where they are – hopefully you'll rest up more easily.

“We permanently feel tired, but we still make sure we go out and have date nights when we can. Otherwise we'd never do anything!”

Ash, 30

Sex, hugs and mock 'n' lol

One of my favourite anecdotes from a friend is when she and her husband had sex for the first time post-birth. It was four months later and they mustered up the courage to give it a go. She describes the hilarity of trying to quietly get down and dirty accompanied by the unexpected soundtrack of their cooing newborn in the Moses basket at the bottom of the bed! I didn't dare ask if they 'finished' the deed, but I think most parents can empathise with the slightly challenging aspect of spontaneous sex. If you haven't had to wedge the bathroom door shut with your foot as Mummy and Daddy 'have a quick grownup chat' then you're lucky.

And then there's 'scheduling it in' sex. Is there anything less sexy than 'booking' your other half in for a quick one with as much phwoar appeal as booking the car in for an MOT? Sometimes needs must, though, so if suggesting some bedroom action a week on Sunday means you're more likely to actually get it on as opposed to not, then I say do what you gotta do.

AUGUST — WEEKLY PLANNER

MON 4pm MOT	FRI
TUE	SAT Dinner Pat + Tim
WED 8.30 Docs	SUN "Sexy time"
THU * Parents evening	notes: dry cleaning?

Some couples manage to maintain a healthy and active sex life pre- and post-having kids, and when I ask them how they make this happen it seems to come down to a mutual desire to appreciate and connect with their partner, not just sexual gratification, as you might think.

Sex is so multi-layered. It's about satisfying those physical urges, of course, but it's also about connecting with your partner on a physical and emotional level. A sex life is important – without it you're just housemates. A relationship is underpinned by physical attraction, trust and communication, so even in those testing, knackering, not-feeling-or-looking-my-best moments, it's important you're both meeting each other's needs on a physical level.

It's often not just about the actual act of 'sex' either. Yes, that's rather nice and also the reason you're both proud parents, but many clients tell me they feel misaligned after they've had children, with each partner having different needs. We all need to feel loved and wanted, and making love is very much a part of that, but it's not the only way we can express our love.

Sex after having kids is often an unspoken issue for a lot of couples. She, perhaps, is feeling anxious and self-conscious after everything her body has been through, and he can equally feel a bit like a fish out of water and apprehensive about getting back to it too. It's really common for couples to feel like this.

Put the act of sex to one side and take that pressure off each other. If you're feeling anxious about intercourse, you're hardly going to be feeling turned on and up for it. Quite the opposite – you'll be as uptight as Gordon Ramsey on a swearing ban. Instead, explore other ways to be intimate with no expectation of actual sex. That will usually just happen naturally when it's right.

Rediscover the simple joy of having a proper cuddle on the sofa or in bed. Enjoy being naked together and giving each other massages or backrubs. Have a good snog (something we all seem to lose the passion for several years in, but a good kiss is sexy AF!). Experiment with foreplay, just appreciating one another, and, if you can, have a giggle together along the way – it's a great way to connect. There are more ideas in chapter 8.

Delightfully different – embracing and evolving

Families come in all shapes and sizes, and that starts with you and your partner. However you've come to be a couple, and however you've got your family, it's perfectly unique to you and should be embraced and celebrated.

You may find yourself in a relationship with someone similar to you, perhaps the same race, religion, social upbringing, or you may fall in love with someone quite different from you in life experience. It's always important for each person to be respected for who they are and what they bring to the relationship.

It's a fact, though, that in relationships where the two people have different backgrounds there may be differences between you that cause friction and discord if not communicated and understood. One of the challenges I often come across is around raising children. I am married to a Sicilian, and much of what drew me to him were his Italian culture and values – family, fun and food! – but as our relationship blossomed differences in our upbringing and cultures (I guess you'd call me white British middle class) surfaced when it came to our ideas on bringing up children.

Typically, Italian kids eat with their family come what may and go to bed really late – it's part of their social culture. I'm a bit of a 'fish fingers for tea at 5pm in front of the telly' and 'in bed, lights out at 7pm' kinda mum. Hmm, this was something we had to discuss and work out and compromise on, and fortunately we did quickly.

I have a client who married into a Jewish family and he has learnt to appreciate and respect the various religious festivals and traditions that come with having a Jewish wife, and now children, who all follow the faith. Another client, who is British, is married to a Polish woman who insists on only speaking in her native language to their children, often leaving him feeling left out, and another client is in a relationship where there are different opinions around discipline.

There are also many differences in relationships for other reasons. You may have grown up in different parts of the country; one of you may be a city lover, the other a country bumpkin at heart. You might have grown up surrounded by strong political views or supporting a certain football team. You may come from plenty of money or not have a pot to pee in. You may have strong opinions on schooling or preferences on hobbies. Every family is different and each of our upbringings is unique.

All families are a wonderful, rich cocktail of traditions and teachings, so it means communicating what's important to you, and upholding your values and beliefs. It also requires respect and compromise where necessary to ensure you and your growing family are all on the same page and everyone knows what's expected of them.

Step families

Step families, or blended families as they are most commonly referred to, are an ever-growing family demographic and, much like the family scenarios already discussed, require communication and boundaries to ensure everyone is on the same page.

I have many friends and clients in second or third marriages that involve children from previous relationships and the challenges faced could almost be a book in itself. Some families nail it and everything slots together beautifully, but others really struggle and that's also perfectly understandable. Two people's decision to be together doesn't automatically mean that everyone else associated is going to be as enamoured.

According to the Office for National Statistics there are over half a million blended families with dependent children in the UK and nearly a third of these families have three children or more. As wonderful as that can be for some, it's challenging for others. A couple deciding to move in together with their children from previous relationships (or perhaps only one has kids) is a big step for everyone involved and should always be treated with sincerity, empathy and respect.

It's not just a challenge for the children to adapt to their new way of life, but also you, the couple, who are juggling your own feelings, your own kids if you have them *and* your stepkids – it's a lot for any relationship to go through.

I have a colleague who went literally from zero to trio. She purposefully decided that she didn't want her own children from quite a young age, but as irony would have it, she fell in love with a wonderful man who has three daughters from a previous relationship. The nature of the set-up means the children spend the majority of time with their father, which meant she had to adapt very quickly to the notion of caring and being responsible for a 'readymade' family. He came as a package. And she made a choice to embrace them all – or walk away. Has it been easy? Hell no, but it's a work in progress.

I know plenty of other couples who have remarried and guided their families into wonderfully vibrant, loving, blended families, and they all tell me that the key ingredient is 'time'. Have a strategy before you all move in together where ground rules, routines and boundaries are openly discussed and established. As a couple it's absolutely key to be united in order for the family to start on the right foot. It takes time for everyone to adapt to being in a new family set-up, so be realistic that there may be teething problems, territorial conflicts and emotional tugs of war within your family and your relationship. Also, be mindful of any exes still in the picture due to children and tread carefully.

Keep things calm, be patient and be purposeful with communication. Lay down any ground rules within your couple as well as with the kids. Allow everyone to have a say where appropriate and, as everyone adjusts to the new family dynamic, you can enjoy the diversity and fun that being together brings.

Family time vs couple time

Kids are undoubtedly testing for any relationship, but amongst the tears, tantrums and tearing your hair out with worry, they are the most wonderful precious blessing. They really are. Many couples feel stronger and more united as a result of becoming parents, and, like everything in life, when challenges occur you face them head on – keep learning, and keep growing. You won't always get it right, but no one ever does. There is no such thing as a perfect parent or perfect partner, you just have to be good enough.

It's important to carve out time for everyone in a family. You want time with the kids to enjoy them, teach them and nurture them with love, affection and boundaries, but it's also just as important to nurture and protect your relationship, and give the same level of priority to each other.

As well as a parenting plan so the family is all on the same page and running as smoothly as possible, make sure you factor yourselves in that too and unapologetically schedule in 'couple time'. Whatever you need to do to make that happen, do it. What options do you have available to you? What would you like to do? And when?

One of my go-to tools to establish this and keep you on track is the GROW model, which I was taught years ago in my coaching training. Work as a team, a couple, and write down your mission statement to ensure you put the spotlight on your relationship regularly.

You and me, me and you

To create your own couple time and keeping growing as a partnership, fill in the answers to the following:

G – what is the Goal? Write down your couple goal in a positive 'Here's where we're heading' statement, for example, 'We will give each other quality time every week.'

R – what is the Reality of this situation currently? Write down any obstacles, challenges, and present thoughts and feelings in relation to the goal.

O – what Options are there to help the goal become a new reality? Who can you call upon to help with the kids? What needs to happen? What resources and ideas do you have?

W – where there's a Will, there's a way! How much do you want to reach your goal? What will it mean to you and your relationship? Is it worth it?

Most couples feel the strain of parenting and without a doubt it moves a relationship into a whole new phase. It's hard work, and also gloriously rewarding and enriching. As long as you hold your relationship in the highest regard, take time to reconnect and appreciate each other, and treat each other as king or queen, then your life together will absolutely become even more wonderful as a couple AND as a family.

5

FOR BETTER, FOR WORSE

Groundhog day

'I do.' Two words so full of giddy promise, trepidation and hope. I can vouch from personal experience that there is nothing more sweaty-palm-inducing than standing face to face with your fiancé and reciting your marriage vows. No matter how much (or little) time and planning has gone into the big day, the moment when you legally declare your love and commitment for another is about as big as it gets. It's the start of a whole new life phase and one which requires teamwork.

Marriage or commitment vows are the most public declarations of love and a pledge to be united, but of course plenty of people forgo the big do and 'piece of paper' altogether and commit to each other in their own way. According to the Office for National Statistics, in 2018 cohabiting couples were the fastest growing 'couple' demographic, with an increase of over 25% in the last decade. Same sex couple families have also grown by more than 50% since 2015. So nowadays living together as a couple, perhaps having children, regardless of your legal marital status, is the main measure – and test – of a relationship.

However you affirm your commitment to each other, it's nigh on impossible to sustain the carefree, starry-eyed first few months or years of a relationship, so the first thing is to give yourself a break if things aren't quite as romantic and lustful as they were in the earlier stages. You couldn't really have foreseen the eye-rolling and huffing that threatens to fog over that wedding day memory several years down the line.

By their very nature, long-term relationships won't always be full-on fun and will sometimes seems more mundane, and what's important is learning to handle those times, recognising what's great about your relationship and not thinking that the grass is greener elsewhere.

Relationships have their ups and downs, their gripes and their groans. Having a realistic perspective on when things might be a little less jazz hands will help you work through those moments without wanting to just throw in the towel and trade your current partner in for a different model.

As a relationship settles down into a more day-to-day rhythm, the initial gloss wears off and a routine and pattern of behaviour develops. And that's OK. Life living together is not just romping around under satin sheets. At some point the loo will need cleaning, the milk in the fridge replenishing and the bills paying. These more mundane – let's be honest, boring – parts of being a couple are far from sexy, but they're real and needed in order to function as a couple and as a family. And given the right attitude and 'reframing' they can be really helpful in strengthening you as a couple.

As a counsellor, lots of people come to me several years into their marriage, complaining that their relationship is 'dead' and they feel 'taken for granted' or like a 'glorified servant'. Respect, affection and communication has waned and needs some serious attention to bring things back to a more agreeable place. Klaxon alert – this is also the time when a wandering eye and cheating can happen, especially if one half feels the need to escape the humdrum of homelife in search of something more 'exciting'. We'll be looking at infidelity later in the book, but in this chapter we'll look at how to put the focus back on your current relationship.

Hey good lookin', what ya got cookin'

My favourite love guru, the anthropologist Dr Helen Fisher, breaks falling in love down into lust, romance and attachment. In a similar way, relationships require lots of ingredients and for me a good one mainly consists of the following three components: friendship, connection and attraction.

Together these make up what should hopefully be a loving, happy relationship. But how many of us actually put in the effort to focus on these key ingredients to ensure our relationship stays strong and fulfilled?

Let's look at these ingredients more closely. A loving relationship is:

Friendship: Warmth, compassion, trust, respect, interest, communication, love

Connection: Empathy, sharing of values, attachment, shared interests, commitment

Attraction: Physical attraction, sexual desire, closeness, admiration, pride

If you look at these again, you'll see that in reality any of these elements can be placed against any of the three ingredients needed to create a fulfilling relationship. They all blend and overlap in one big melting pot and without one – in other words, unless all three are in play – the relationship takes on a very different dynamic and will struggle.

Essentially all three of these ingredients are needed for a romantic relationship to work. There will be times when one is more present or dormant than the others, for example if one of you is unwell (and doesn't feel up to much) attraction may temporarily be at a lower level than friendship (where companionship and compassion are more prevalent). You might love doing the same things (connection), but be struggling to appreciate that in each other and find ways to enjoy them together (attraction).

Most of us find that life gets in the way and we forget to prioritise our relationship, but without continual focus and putting the work in to keep all three of the love ingredients plentiful, we run the risk of it being shoved to the bottom of the 'to do' list, along with de-fleaing the cat and putting out the dustbin.

Uh oh, we're in trouble

According to the Office for National Statistics divorce rates in the UK have declined over the past few decades, which is great news. The average age for getting a divorce or breaking up is 46.4yrs old for men and 43.9yrs old for women – perhaps we can understand where that old cliché about having a mid-life crisis at 40 comes from – with the lowest rates of divorce in the 20- to 30-year-old age bracket.

Given that the average age for getting married in the UK has now increased to 35 for a woman and 38 for a man in opposite sex couples, which make up the majority, and 37 for women and 40 for men in same sex couples, this gives us a heads-up on why that average age for divorce is where it is. It would appear that a few years in, the shine of the honeymoon period has worn off and the relationship is declared over.

But if you look at the stats for the older generation of 60+, the rates of divorce sharply decline, so what does that tell us? That they're getting on now and can't be arsed to change things? That the thought of being single and on dating apps isn't quite their cup of tea? Or could it be that their relationship has been up, down, evolved and back again, and seen the test of time? I like to believe it's the latter and it's that thinking – of sticking with it, putting in the graft and not throwing in the towel at the first sign of trouble – that I want to discuss in this chapter.

Relationships are never plain sailing and straight forward, and if you think about all the variables at play (health, work, friends and family, finances) it would be weird if they were. However, having a stable, loving relationship has long been shown to help you feel more secure, live longer, deal with stress better, adopt healthier behaviours and have a better sense of purpose. Most of us can identify with that 'groundhog day' feeling – the unchanged loo roll, the unpaid council tax bill lying around on the kitchen worktop, the mess, the nagging, the sitting at opposite ends of the sofa in silence blindly scrolling

Instagram... If any of this sounds familiar, it's time to step up, shake yourself off and refocus on what's important – which is your relationship. It's worth it.

Alarm bells

There are, of course, some situations when sticking with it is not in your best interests and cutting your losses is absolutely the right thing to do. If your relationship has become toxic, abusive or there are signs (such as excessive drinking or threatened violence) that it could become so – basically if you feel unsafe in any way – then call someone you trust and leave the situation immediately to keep yourself safe. There is a lot more on this in chapter 8.

What seems to be the problem?

There is no clear time marker for when a relationship might run into trouble. Some people have a right royal bicker before the ink has even dried on the marriage certificate, others leave it a few years until the honeymoon sparkle has worn off.

Never measure yourself against anybody else's relationship. In my experience the old adage that you never know what goes on behind closed doors is absolutely true. You might think the So-and-sos from down the road are #TotallyLovedUp, but you're only seeing what they want you to see – a representation of themselves as a couple. They may be anything but perfect, and they may be working hard to get there, but you won't see the personal challenges that they are dealing with in private.

The reason for that is it's just not appropriate to share some things with all and sundry. A partnership is unique and highly personal, and there are certain aspects that should remain private and sacred to you both. Talking about personal matters such as finances and sexual performance, for instance, is crossing the line of respect and 'our business'. We all have issues and make mistakes, and whereas it's OK to share any issues and gain counsel from trusted friends or professionals (especially if you're concerned over anything which compromises your wellbeing and safety), it's important to work together to identify any problems and work on a solution as a couple.

> 'Every time we have a row she goes to her mum and basically slags me off. It makes me feel so insecure and angry.'
>
> Dan, 29

There are many reasons why a relationship might get into difficulty, and being open and honest about the cause of you butting heads is key to working out what can be done to resolve them. Remember the rules of a good conversation:

- Talk to each other in a calm and measured way.
- Listen to what the other is saying.
- Don't interrupt each other.
- Respect what the other has said even if you don't agree with it.
- Work calmly together to figure out how you can see things moving forward.

All of the above should help you find the healthiest way to address an issue, but you might also benefit from seeking outside help too. Individual and couples counselling and therapy is hugely helpful, and many people I know and have worked with rave about how it has been a relationship saviour. There's more about therapy and what it's about later in the book.

So what are the most common problems most couples face?

Money: Some reports suggest this is the number one cause of relationship breakdown. A lot of couples have different attitudes and habits around their finances. Earning, saving vs spending, not having enough of it and how to share it – all can be problematic if you're not on the same page.

Compatibility: Once the honeymoon phase has faded away, many couples realise they don't have the same values and that can cause a huge problem when it comes to expectations of how you want to live as a couple. For example, you might have different values (or definitions) of how you like to relax – one might love chilling on the sofa, the other hiking up a mountain.

Lack of communication: Couples often blame their relationship issues on not being able to communicate properly. This can result in unproductive arguing, withdrawing (avoiding) and stonewalling (evading). It is sometimes about having (or not having) the right communication skills (there's more about this in chapter 3), but it can also be deeply rooted in problems that the couple aren't talking about.

Conflict: Constant arguing can be toxic and is utterly miserable for both involved. It could be about anything – trust issues, roles, power struggles – but if arguments are left unresolved things are unlikely to improve.

Intimacy: Changes in libido, conflicting sex drives and sexual function, and lack of attraction are just some of the challenges that can hinder a partnership, but intimacy also extends outside the bedroom with emotional closeness being a huge part of what makes a relationship tick. Holding hands, an affectionate kiss hello, a supportive hand on the back, saying 'I love you', a shoulder massage or a foot rub – these are all examples of being intimate without having sex.

Infidelity: Cheating on your partner is one of the biggest offences you can commit in a marriage. There's the physical act of cheating, but equally hurtful is emotionally cheating on your partner with someone else. It might cause irreparable damage, but it can sometimes be worked through if both of you are willing to forgive and work on repairing the relationship.

Interfering in-laws: We've all heard the 'mother-in-law' jokes, but overzealous and interfering family members can cause a huge issue for a couple. Power struggles, unwanted advice and conflicting values can all rock even the strongest couples.

These are some of the most widely reported issues that crop up in marriages and long-term relationships, and unless they are addressed and resolved, the end result can sadly be divorce or separation. The final chapter in this book is about recognising when a relationship has reached that point, is unsalvageable, and it's time to move on. It's realistic that we look at this outcome, because unfortunately a lot of couples have and will find themselves in that position. The good news is plenty can be done to stop such a drastic event ever taking place in your relationship, so we're going to work on prevention and early intervention.

How to deal with the deal-breakers

As highlighted, money matters, compatibility, communication, conflict, intimacy, infidelity, interfering in-laws – these are the biggies that are often the cause of a relationship going sour. However, there are some key conversations you can have to help stage an intervention before things get too far down the road of no turning back.

Money: Broach the subject by inviting the conversation in a non-confrontational way, such as, 'When it's convenient to us both, can we have a chat about our finances?' Sharing a financial goal, such as, 'I would love us to save up for a holiday,' also helps to work out where your heads are at, how each other feels about that goal and what needs to happen to reach it.

Compatibility: I talk a lot in this book about values, and you need to explore them to work out what's important to you both and ensure you're on the same page. You may both value recreational downtime, for instance, but if your definitions of what that looks like are polar opposites (one wants to chill, one wants to climb Ben Nevis), then it's going to be a problem. Try any of the values-based exercises in this book (have a look at chapter 1) and suggest you address it together.

Lack of communication: It doesn't always have to be the big conversations. In fact, it's the small talk that's just as important. Sharing everyday experiences, chatting about a podcast you've heard or a TV show you're enjoying can be just as valuable in keeping connected. Make time for each other to chat over the big and the small stuff, and, if it's needed, schedule in downtime together to talk – the simplest of acts yet often the hardest and most neglected.

Conflict: It's really important when there's conflict to switch your mindset to a useful, productive one in order to work through it. Don't place blame, drag up old arguments or list all the things that annoy you about your partner. It'll only serve to create even more atmosphere. Instead, focus on the present and where you're heading. Discuss where you'd like things to get to and what needs to happen to get there amicably. Be open to listening, learning and actioning anything which needs to be actioned in order to resolve any issues.

Intimacy: You may have heard the saying 'A couple that plays together, stays together' and there's a lot of truth in this. There are varying degrees of intimacy – physical, emotional, financial – and two big components needed are trust and time. You also have to mutually want it. Work on what you do together outside the bedroom as much as what you do inside it (that's also important though). Share interests, allow yourselves to be vulnerable and talk about any worries, concerns, hopes, dreams etc. It surprises a lot of couples when they reconnect in this way, because it can bring so many positives to a relationship.

Infidelity: As hard as it can be to stay rational, try and communicate together to understand what was behind the act of cheating. Allow each other the space to speak uninterrupted. Each of you needs to take responsibility for your role and actions, and to be held accountable. Each of you may also need physical space and time in order to work out how you feel and any next steps (i.e. counselling, forgiveness, further communication, making changes).

Interfering in-laws: Keep your cool and avoid letting your emotions spill over into unhelpful territory – slagging off your husband's mother to him is rarely going to do you any favours. Be factual about what you're unhappy about and ask for your partner's help to resolve any issues. Agree boundaries together and present them as a united front. Where possible, keep a sense of humour to help diffuse any tension between you both.

There are some deal-breakers that unfortunately can't be worked through – things that are wrong, illegal and cause harm, either physically and/or mentally. It can be difficult to know when to call things a day and it's normal to feel confused and sometimes even conflicted. It's not necessarily an easy solution, and lots of people need support to find the courage in such situations, but in most cases the best course of action is to leave the relationship.

Gaslighting: This is when a partner sows seeds of doubt in your mind that cause you to question your own memory, perception or judgement. The purpose of it is to convince the person being gaslit that they can't trust their own thoughts or instincts. It's a form of psychological manipulation, mental abuse and control, and it's recognised in the UK as domestic abuse and a criminal offence.

Narcissistic behaviours: This is when everything is about them. Narcissists have a constant need for attention and if they don't get it they can get irritated, nasty and resentful. This 'all about me' attitude affects decisions, opinions, choices – basically everything – and the partner's thoughts and feelings are completely ignored. Narcissists also show complete disrespect for other people's boundaries and a common trait is using isolation as a way to gain control over a partner so that they become fully dependent on them.

Sexual abuse: Any unwanted conduct falls under this category. Rape and sexual abuse (no means no), including in a relationship, is a criminal offence.

Coercive control: This is when a pattern of acts deprives someone of their independence. This can include intimidation, humiliation, assaults or threats. The person often feels isolated and dependent on their abuser, which can make it hard to seek help and speak out.

Financial abuse: This is when a partner is restricted or controlled by the other using money. They may keep control over the bank accounts or cards, they might not allow them to spend anything or they might track their spending in a way which makes the victim feel worried or scared.

Physical and verbal abuse: It is a criminal offence to physically or mentally hurt someone. This includes hitting, kicking, throwing things to cause harm, name-calling or using cruel or threatening language.

If you find yourself in any of these situations, or anything else makes you doubt yourself or feel unsafe or unhappy, do seek help so you can take the appropriate steps to improve that situation. You'll find some useful resources and people to contact, should you ever need to, at the end of the book.

Red flags

There are some common warning signs that a relationship may be in trouble. Have a think about your own relationship. Can you spot any of the following that you're guilty of?

Secret squirrel: You start keeping secrets or telling little lies. Perhaps you've stayed late for work drinks, but avoided telling him who with. Maybe you're buying things on the joint account you said you wouldn't. Deliberately keeping secrets for whatever reason only plants seeds of doubt and distrust, raises eyebrows, prompts questions about what you're saying or doing, and can quickly spiral out of control into big lies.

Criticism over compliments: Constructive, well-meant criticism, when politely offered up or asked for, can be a good thing. It serves as feedback to help us all grow and be better people. But if being critical of your other half, and vice versa, is massively outweighing the compliments you give your partner, it's important you readdress this balance immediately. Research tells us that you need five positive comments to outweigh one bad!

Argument groundhog day: We know from chapter 3 how arguing can actually be a really good thing in a relationship. Couples who argue can be happier than those who sweep it under the carpet, but if certain arguments are becoming repetitive with no resolution, then the disconnect needs to be addressed and resolved before you both start just avoiding each other.

Silence is not golden: NOT arguing at all can also be a massive 'we're in trouble' klaxon. Not even bothering to argue or challenge each other about something which is important and matters can be a sign that one (or both) of you have given up. Is there something left to fight for? Silence is often much worse than the alternative of having an important head-to-head heart-to-heart.

Sex drought: It's perfectly normal for the chandelier-swinging sex marathons to ease off once you get into an established relationship, but physical intimacy is important in a healthy and fulfilled couple. Everyone goes through dry periods when it comes to sex, but if you're both fit and healthy adults, having no sex at all may be an issue.

Time out: A healthy relationship is an interdependent one. This is where you have your time together, but you also have your own individual pursuits, friends, interests and so on outside the relationship. If you find you want to spend more time away from your partner and you are making excuses not to be together, this is a major red flag that all is not well.

Wandering eye: There's nothing wrong with platonically admiring someone other than your partner, or occasionally finding another person attractive. What's not OK is having inappropriate thoughts or fantasising about being with them. This is a red flag that you're missing something in your relationship and before you make any moves you may live to regret, use this warning sign as an opportunity to work out what is going on (wrong) in your relationship.

Checking out: If your partner isn't the one you're calling to share good news, or to confide in when you're in trouble or feeling down, then this could be a sign that communication has gone awry and needs some attention.

These warning signs should become part of your marriage SOS toolkit – a checklist to refer to if things get a bit stale or feel shaky with you and your partner. Pinpoint any areas which need urgent attention and some TLC to avoid a whole load of trouble, which will certainly keep brewing if left ignored.

Prevent niggles becoming massive issues by keeping the focus on your relationship, checking in on how you're both feeling, and keeping communication at the forefront of everything you do together – it will all help to keep the red flags at bay. And the good news is, if you work through these challenges, particularly if you catch them early, you'll go on to have an even stronger relationship.

And awareness is key. I've had clients come to me worried that they were having zero bedroom action and pals who had started to keep secrets from their other halves out of fear of getting an arsey reaction. In every instance they were concerned about what this meant for the state of their relationships. The really good thing is that they'd recognised and confronted within themselves these 'red flags' early. Armed with counsel from me (the same advice you're reading in this book), they were able to take positive next steps and address their worries with their partners.

By communicating and being vulnerable with their partners they were able to explain their feelings and fears, and work on resolutions to ensure they both felt heard and valued, and fulfilled within their relationship. The couples ended up feeling much happier.

Remember – prevention and early intervention is key. Look out for the red flags, work together to resolve any flash points, and your relationship will go from strength to strength.

Getting to know you... again

It may seem obvious to suggest spending time together, as a couple, simply talking. But you might be surprised how many couples *don't*. Life gets so busy. We become consumed with all the other 'noise' that reverberates around us and we're guilty of shoving those we love the most down the bottom of the pecking order when it comes to having a jolly good chat about the stuff that matters. I'm not talking about household bills and who's picking the kids up from school, either. I'm talking about your partnership.

A great way of keeping the red flags at bay is to keep checking in with each other and reminding yourselves why you're together. Being in a relationship should always be through choice, not need. Schedule a 'date night' or, if that's a bit too fancy, a time when you can be together without interruption and verbally agree that it's a time for you both to reconnect.

Only (re)connect

Get some blank cards or Post-it notes and each write the following sentences about the other, filling in the ending:

- When I first saw you I thought...
- The nicest thing you've ever done for me is...
- You make me smile when you...
- I love you because...
- We make a great couple because...

When you're done, read out the sentences to each other in turn and enjoy the positive reactions. It's a great exercise to reconnect and remind yourselves why you're together and how you feel about one another.

Don't sweat the small stuff

Up to this point we've covered a lot of the big things – money, sex, in-laws – that can cause major relationship upset. But sometimes big issues start from smaller niggles that begin as an itch, then turn into an irk, then explode into a full-blown issue – that routine stuff that makes us tut under our breath in annoyance. In the poll I put out recently on social media asking about the top niggles in relationships, I was inundated with frustrations, and the same things came up again and again. Talk about opening the floodgates!

It was actually quite astonishing how many niggles and frustrations stemmed from the same day-to-day events, and yet hardly anyone had made steps to confront these issues within their couples! In no particular order, these are the things they reported:

- Feeling taken for granted
- Feeling underappreciated for doing household chores
- Laziness
- General household mess

- Gender roles
- Parenting differences
- Phone/laptop/PS4 obsession
- Not being listened to and crap communication
- Honesty and trust issues
- Jealousy – re. solo time, attention from others
- Failure to use the dishwasher
- Toilet cleanliness
- Insecurities, i.e. ex-partners and body hang-ups
- Questionable hygiene
- Lack of regular sex/affection (kissing, hugging, foreplay)
- Having different priorities, i.e. friends/in-laws over partner
- Money – rogue spending
- Interfering in-laws
- Snoring
- Bed hogging
- Gross or loud eating
- Foul habits, i.e. farting, feetpicking, bogey-eating
- Lack of compromise
- Nagging
- Childcare sharing
- Wait for it... breathing!

Now, I'm sure, like me, the list raised a smile of recognition. It seems we are all riled by the same things. It's the club no one really wants to be a member of, but there is certainly comfort and solidarity in knowing that it really isn't just you experiencing these gripes.

But do we simply accept that this is the way it is and just suck it up? Or should we do something about it and work on ways to feel less aggrieved and more agreeable? Well, *obviously* I'm going to say the latter! A relationship is supposed to be supportive, equal and respectful, and even though we enjoy a good moan about the nagging, lack of nookie and feeling like an unpaid housekeeper, it's time we did something about it.

> “Why do women always say they're fine when they're clearly not! It's infuriating!”
>
> Matt, 31

I'm fine!

Communication is the name of the game. As you'll know from chapter 4, one of my favourite sayings is, 'Assumption is the mother of all f**k ups.' If we're not actually letting our partner know in an appropriately communicated way (i.e. not by screeching, blaming, yelling or moaning) that there is a problem, then how are they supposed to know what we're annoyed about?

But if these day-to-day niggles are allowed to multiply, everything just gets worse. It's like a chain reaction too. Nagging can lead to no sex... no sex can lead to feeling underappreciated... feeling underappreciated can lead to jealousy... jealousy can lead to more intense nagging and so on. It's all one rather unpleasant vicious circle.

So let's nip it in the bud. Let's communicate properly.

You might not be a natural talker – lots of people aren't and that's OK – but have a think about how you can communicate with your partner so that they will listen to what you have to say. What are you unhappy with? Why are you unhappy with it? What would you like your partner to do to help you feel more XYZ? Some good ways of communicating your needs are:

Write a letter or email: I love this method. It rarely fails to help get across what you're feeling and want to say in a safe, measured, non-confrontational way. Give your letter to your partner and ask them to read it in their own time, away from you, and, when they feel ready, you'd value a response. It's an effective way to get conversations flowing and kick-start any compromises or changes that might need to take place.

Say it with a poem or a song: It might not seem like an obvious way to let your partner know how you're feeling, but poetry and song-writing are hugely powerful in conveying feelings that perhaps the spoken conversational word can't do justice to. Have a go at writing a poem or song yourself or, if that's too tall an order, 'borrow' how you're feeling from a well-known song or poem which can help communicate what *you* want to say.

Leave a voice, text or WhatsApp message: We live in an age when we're glued to our technology. This can cause problems in itself, but it's also a useful way to communicate, particularly when issues arise, before they stew and get out of hand. I'd never recommend a full-blown conversation over text or messaging as things can often get lost in translation with a disconnected 'right to reply' which can cause more frustration. But it can be a good tool to use to tee something up which needs further chatting about at a time convenient to you both.

Talk it out: Many people find it hard to talk, even/especially to their loved one. But practice makes perfect, so choose a good time to chat, forewarn them that you'd like to have a positive talk about some elements of your relationship which you'd like to work on together and, if it helps, make some notes in advance of the chat to keep you on course. There are really helpful communication love hacks in chapter 3 which can help with this, too.

“Sometimes he may take my blunt self as a bad mood, when it's not.”

Lexi, 40

Priority pass

There's an old saying about familiarity breeding contempt. Familiarity also breeds complacency. The definition of complacency is 'a feeling of self-satisfaction and contentment, especially when coupled with an unawareness of danger, trouble of controversy'. One of the most common gripes I get from couples is feeling unappreciated, taken for granted and low down the list of their partner's priorities.

And it's often not a conscious thing. We are all probably guilty of occasionally 'forgetting' about the people in our lives who really matter. How many times have you put in extra effort with new friends or work colleagues, because you want to make a good impression, they don't really know you and you don't want to be misjudged? FOMO (fear of missing out) also plays a huge part. And yet our long-established relationships and friendships are placed at the back of the queue when it comes to prioritising a catch-up.

It seems like such a contradiction, doesn't it? That the people we are supposed to love, cherish and care about the most are the ones we often leave to grapple for the scraps on the floor when it comes to our time, effort and energy.

But why?

It comes down to trust and feeling comfortable. Both are great qualities that are highly important in friendships and relationships, but so many of us become complacent, a little bit too comfy, and assume the other will always be there. When it comes to the relationships that really matter, though, we *should* be prioritising those over all others.

Our meaningful relationships are the ones which give us stability, strength, energy, love, acceptance, encouragement and a safe space to be authentic. But for that to happen we need to be tuned into our partners *always*. I've lost track of the number of people who've told me they don't feel prioritised in their relationship. They feel effort has diminished on both sides – you're not going to keep putting in effort if it's not being reciprocated – and complacency, laziness and familiarity have overtaken the core values of the relationship, i.e. making the other person feel loved, special and happy.

Checking in on your relationship is really key to keeping it healthy and happy, and ensuring you prioritise your partner above all others will never fail to serve you well. Even if you have children, they should know and see how important and respected their parents are to each other. It serves as terrific role-modelling and teaches them to respect the boundaries around the sanctity of a committed relationship.

Yes, life is busy and there are so many elements that need our attention we can take our eye off the ball at times. All of us benefit from a little reminder and helping hand when it comes to putting our partner at the top of the priority list.

One of my favourite suggestions is to prioritise your partner and their needs as you would a doctor's appointment or a job interview or a school pick-up. We would never miss one of those. We prioritise them because the consequences of not doing so could be catastrophic. Not prioritising your relationship, if left for too long, could have a similar fate.

And much like an important doctor's or dentist's appointment is an essential part of keeping well, it's the same for your relationship. Giving time with each other as much importance will ensure you're giving each other much-needed focus and TLC.

Get your diary out, dust off that wall calendar and pop in some couple time at frequent intervals. Treat your 'us time' as having the highest importance. Plan simple things like going for a walk together, as well as date nights, and enjoy the rewards of actively prioritising your partner – and your relationship.

> “Every Thursday night without fail my wife and I go for a bite to eat at the local pub. We always eat and drink the same thing – steak and chips with a beer – and we have a good talk. It's great for checking in on what each other's been up to or if there's anything on our minds.”
>
> Gary, 42

The chores wars

Without a doubt, one of the top moans couples seem to have about each other is the division of household chores. If I'm honest, it's mainly women who are exasperated at their men for doing basically bugger all in comparison to the pack horse they feel they've become, with the majority of tasks being heaped on their shoulders.

But we need to be fair here. There are also plenty of guys who are fed up with being unfairly stereotyped, and who in actual fact do a hell of a lot more than their missuses around the house and for their relationship. There really is no right or wrong on what you agree to do (or not do) within your couple and home, as long as you both agree with it. Equality in the workplace may be improving (flexible working, paternity leave etc.), but when it comes to the home, it seems a lot of couples are stuck in a 1950s time warp of 'woman does the housework' and 'man brings home the dosh' – and for many this is breeding contempt.

'He's so lazy.' I hear this time and time again. 'She's a total nag.' I hear this just as much... and yet I heard the same remarks from my elderly grandparents who came from a generation where traditionally women *didn't* work and men *did*. Back in the 1940s and 50s it was just how it was in the main. My grandmother cooked, cleaned and looked after my grandfather, and he worked hard, ensuring they had money in the bank, but there wouldn't have even been a *suggestion* of him ironing his own shirts or bleaching the lavvy! Hell would have sooner frozen over.

Roles were a little more clearly defined due to the times they were living in then, but fast forward the best part of a century, and the same attitudes still largely apply. The problem is that with men and women now having parity in terms of careers, financial status and opportunities, there is a problem when it comes to balancing the running of the home.

In a heterosexual relationship, household responsibilities still tend to fall on the woman's shoulders, whether she likes it or not. Nothing pisses us off more than chores and who does what.

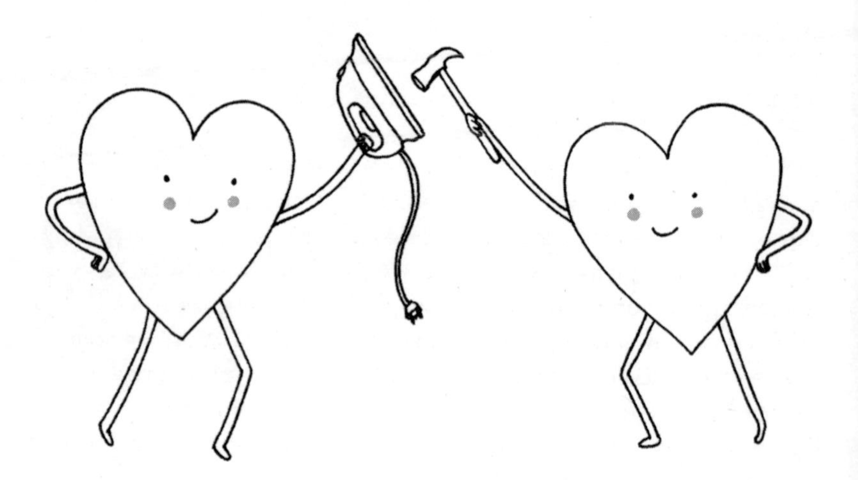

Pink jobs or blue jobs?

Pink jobs and blue jobs are often how they're referred to – how wonderfully stereotypical! But for donkey's years household jobs have been unofficially categorised into gender-specific roles. We all know which is which, but for the avoidance of doubt here are some of them:

Blue jobs

- Taking the bins out
- Doing the gardening
- Washing the car
- Unblocking the toilet
- Putting up shelves
- Any other general DIY activities

Pink jobs

- Washing
- Cooking
- Cleaning
- Shopping
- Ironing
- Remembering birthdays, school bags etc.

It's all incredibly clichéd, isn't it, but as much as we like to think we've moved on from this rather traditional way of life, evidence tells me we actually haven't. Sure, the lines are more blurred with pink jobs overlapping with blue and vice versa, but for the majority of heterosexual couples, these gender roles are still steeped in the past!

Let's be clear, if it works for you then there is actually nothing wrong with having pink and blue jobs. I know plenty of couples who are extremely happy with this set-up. In fact, I have a BFF who has recently given up her job and emigrated with her husband and children, and while he solely works and earns the dollars, she is a proud (and incredible) 'stay at home mum', running the household and rearing their children. The roles within their marriage are clearly defined, it's balanced and it works really well for them – it's teamwork.

But I also know many more who are aren't so content, and the reason tends to be that the women are juggling careers and children *as well as* the day-to-day jobs that running a home and family entails. It's when the balance is off within a couple that trouble and dissatisfaction will start to brew.

I have a client who is a partner in a law firm. Her husband also has a demanding job and they have three children. They met at university, and really value and respect the hard work the other puts into their career. However, from the moment the ring went on the finger and they uttered 'I do,' most of the household and family organisation 'automatically' fell to her. It wasn't a conscious thing from either of them, it just sort of happened. And it really gets her goat!

When did we learn this conditioned behaviour, ladies? At school? Passed down the generations like a family heirloom no one really wants but begrudgingly accepts? It's baffling how the majority of women I know in relationships feel they do way more than their partners do in all areas, and it's almost accepted as a socially conditioned 'given'. We *joke* how women can multitask and some men just can't.

Then there's the mental labour too. Remembering your mother-in-law's birthday, buying his *and* your family's Christmas presents, ordering new school shoes for the kids, being the tooth fairy, organising the dentist's appointments, sending off for passport renewals... the list is endless.

But how many people hold themselves accountable? How many are guilty of not laying out the boundaries and communicating reasonable expectations of each other? I'll stick my hand up and say that looking at my own set-up, I often just cracked on with X, Y and Z because it was quicker, easier and invariably done to my (more thorough) standards. I made a rod for my own back and actually had myself to blame a lot of the time. I realised that if I just kept taking over by default and didn't give my husband the responsibility and trust in his efforts then *why would he* make a concerted effort to do the things I automatically did?

I'll always remember the day I realised we needed to sort this. We were getting the children ready for the day and my husband was dressing our son. Being a typical three-year-old at the time he'd thrown a tantrum, insisting on wearing his superhero t-shirt, which was in the washing basket filthy dirty. I heard my husband say, 'Sorry, you can't wear that today. Mummy hasn't washed it yet.' An innocent comment, but one which irked me big time! We *both* worked, we were *both* responsible for our kids, and yet without any discussion at all, the task of being chief clothes washer had been automatically assigned to me purely because of my gender – and I was equally responsible for going along with the assumption.

In recent years my husband and I have addressed the pink and blue jobs. We now refer to them as purple jobs, which certainly makes things feel a lot more equal. We staked our claim on what we felt was fair mainly based on skill. I hate ironing and he's a whizz with an iron so that's his gig; I genuinely love cleaning so that's mine; and we both like cooking so we take it in turns. Bins, car washing, gardening, laundry washing are all purple jobs and fair game. It's very much about not assuming the other one will do it, playing fair and not dodging it! Instead, we check what needs doing, consider what else each other is juggling, and then dish out the chores accordingly.

Whose job is it anyway?'

You might balk at the rather archaic notion of gender roles and who does what around the house, but outdated or not, the fact that *so* many people complain about this particular issue means it's too real to ignore. Pink, blue, purple... whatever. What it's really about is sharing household responsibilities fairly between you and your partner. Here are a few things to consider first:

Value time equally: When you're dividing up chores it's important to consider what else each of you has going on both inside and outside the home, so your time is valued equally. School runs, shopping, working, paying bills, childcare... so many variables to consider. If one partner works full-time and the other part-time, it might be reasonable to suggest the part-timer takes on a few more of the household and family tasks. It's also important to acknowledge there are only so many hours in the day and everyone is entitled to some downtime. Respecting each other's free time is also super-important.

Get on the same page: Expectations need to be clear and realistic. Most people have their own ideas – or standards – when it comes to chores. You might like to hoover the house once a day, but your partner might think once a week is fine. Your partner may prefer the bed linen changed once a week and you may feel that once a fortnight is more than OK... Find a middle ground that is realistic and satisfactory to you both. When you're sorting out chores make sure everyone is on the same page about what a task entails – it will save frustration and resentment.

Rope in the kids: If you have offspring who are vaguely old enough to help out, then draw up some jobs for them to complete, too. Making the beds, filling the dishwasher, putting shoes away... it all helps and getting them to do their bit means they won't expect the 'magic cleaning fairy' to do everything.

Call in the professionals: If you're really not getting anywhere and the stress is putting unnecessary pressure on your relationship, consider outsourcing. Hiring a cleaning firm to give the house a spruce once a week, someone in to do the ironing, a food delivery subscription service or signing up for shopping deliveries can help out enormously – and gives you the time this creates together doing something much nicer.

Job on

- Get a wall calendar and create some 'job cards' for a lucky dip.
- Write down on separate cards all the jobs, chores and responsibilities that need to be addressed.
- Be sure to think outside the box. There are the main chores, but there are also the typical 'mum labour' jobs that are equally tiresome and mindbogglingly overwhelming, such as shopping around for insurance renewals, paying the window cleaner, topping up the kids' school dinner money fund, taking the cat to the vet... the mental merry-go-round never stops.
- As you would a game of snap, share the cards out equally face down. Then each reveal your set of jobs.
- Do this each week, fortnight or month – whatever you both feel is appropriate to freshen the responsibilities up – and agree to stick to the tasks. Put the tasks on the wall calendar by each person's name, so it's clear for all to see and there's no room for 'Oh but I thought that was your job this week' confusion or job-dodging.
- Should the jobs need reallocating at any point (circumstances can change, of course), you can discuss how to support each other best.

“I feel like I'm the only one doing anything around the house. He always says it's because he 'works', but I also have a full-time job!”

Anthea, 37

Get off your bl**dy phone!

I couldn't complete this chapter without addressing one of the other main gripes that seems to cause unrest in relationships – phones and tech.

We live in a digital age – and thank goodness we do for so many great reasons. Being able to chat to loved ones living on the other side of the world, working from home, the digital 'babysitter', social media, online shopping, the list is endless. But there is also the less positive side of always being 'on'. It takes some discipline to come off technology, social media, emails etc., and to set boundaries and time away from having your face glued to a screen 24/7.

There are so many justifications for having your smartphone permanently attached to your hand, ear and eye. I've heard them all: 'Oh but I'm expecting a really important work email,' 'I'm in a live eBay auction and I don't want to miss out,' 'so and so is about to do an Instagram Live'... These 'reasons' are all well and good, but without a doubt, the over-use of technology and phones has become a massive thing. And it's rapidly become the 'third wheel' in a couple, with too much time spent looking down connecting with cyberspace, as opposed to looking up and seeing who and what you have around you in real life.

As we do with all other areas of relationships, it's about setting reasonable expectations and boundaries, and communicating effectively, i.e. not screaming across the kitchen 'Will you get off your bloody phone!'

Phones are addictive. That's a fact! They are designed to draw us in, and with all the little beeps, flashes, notifications and 'likes' giving our brains that hit of the happy hormone dopamine, we're IN, hook, line and sinker.

But unless we're self-aware and giving ourselves proper downtime from being plugged into our devices, we run the risk of neglecting those around us. We don't give our full attention to those we're actually physically with and it can start to feel like our virtual life is valued more than our real life together.

> “He'd rather sit on his phone than play with the children. He has a problem, but he can't see it!”
>
> Jack, 35

First of all, identify if tech, phones and devices, have become a problem and are driving a wedge between you both. Look out for the following signs:

Distracted: We can all be guilty of doing a few things at once, but if you or your partner are constantly scrolling through Twitter or Instagram during a conversation or when concentration is meant to be on something else, it's not just rude, it's an issue.

Unaware of a problem: If you or your partner gets irritable if you can't log on (wifi issues), you feel anxious if the phone gets misplaced, your mood changes dramatically due to something on your phone, i.e. comparing yourself to someone on social media or receiving an annoying email during antisocial hours, or switching off literally and mentally is a massive challenge, all this is a sign that boundaries need to be set around phone usage.

Feeling rejected: If your sex life is suffering due to phone scrolling in the marital bed, or one of you is feeling rejected due to an electronic device holding your partner's attention instead of you, or you basically just feel ignored, it's completely fair enough to feel pissed off.

Others have noticed: Perhaps friends, family or colleagues have made comments about how often the devices are in use? Perhaps it's just a little joke here and there, but if it's being noticed by others, then it's certainly something to think about.

So what can we do about it? Let me reassure you, you will not be alone in juggling the technology in your relationship and family. As we evolve with the digital age, it's important we learn boundaries around tech usage to ensure our relationships keep thriving and we feel valued.

Scrollin' scrollin' scrollin'

Instead of wanting to smash your partner's phone against a brick wall in frustration at the constant mindless scrolling, agree to work together to come up with a set of 'tech rules' so you both feel respected, free to do what you *need* to do and valued within your couple time.

Be honest: As you would with any conflict, find a mutually agreeable time to calmly chat. Articulate how tech time is making you feel, but refrain from being aggressive or using accusatory language, because otherwise they'll shut down and become defensive. Highlight how much more positive things would be if tech boundaries were set and adhered to.

No tech zone: Agree when devices, apps, emails etc. *need* to be used (i.e. perhaps your partner works for an international company and is required to be online at antisocial hours) and when they can be put away or turned off. Ban devices in the bedroom full stop. Bedrooms should be for two things, sleeping and sex, and phones massively scupper both activities! Also remove phones from the dinner table. It's rude and a distraction from giving everyone at the table your full attention. Agree a place to keep all your devices so they can physically be out of sight with any temptation to check them removed.

Change settings: Phones, computers, tablets... they're all wired to let us know when someone wants to get our attention. That ping, beep or flash on the screen grabs our attention like a laser beam! The dopamine hit has become all too alluring. Change your settings to turn off sound, notifications and vibrations, and if there is someone who really might need to get hold of you, let them know to ring you instead.

It's often not until we've made a concerted effort to make changes that we realise how necessary and useful they are. Digital devices are great, but not as great as the natural dopamine and other feel-good chemical hit of getting fresh with your loved one.

> "He's always working and never knows when to switch off – it drives me mad and we always bicker about it."
>
> Rosa, 38

Acceptance – warts and all

The very title of this chapter sums it all up really. For better, for worse – because your relationship *will* have ups and downs. To expect anything else would be naïve and unhelpful, but it's all about how we embrace the great stuff and deal with more challenging aspects as they present themselves. That's how we build and keep maintaining resilience in ourselves and our most important relationships.

Some relationships, with every good will in the world, can't quite make it down the long road to happily ever after and that's OK. It's important to recognise when all the effort and trying is hitting a dead end – we'll talk more about this in the last chapter – but among all the frustrations and tough times, as long as there is an ember burning away your relationship has every chance of standing the test of time. You just have to both want it and put in the work – and on occasion eat a big piece of humble pie.

Relationships also need a heavy dollop of acceptance. Yes, you might find your mother-in-law irritating as hell, his farts and toilet habits may repulse you at times, and her incessant need to go out with the girls may drive you up the wall... but that's what makes a relationship real. What a unique privilege yours is. Cherish it – and each other – always.

6
THE S WORD

Let's talk about sex... baby

It's fair to say that the topic of sex is always pretty cringe. Talking about sex is up there with discussing death, finances and incontinence – uncomfortable. It's awkward, but it's important that, when things go a little awry, we talk about it. Ironically, *talking* about sex can be about as *unsexy* as it comes, but we're all grown-ups now, so take your fingers out of your ears and let's have 'the chat'.

I'm going to make an assumption here that when you were younger the topic of sex wasn't an easy one. We are socially conditioned to find 'it' awkward and embarrassing from the moment we hit puberty, and our form tutor gets out the cucumbers and condoms to 'practise' being safe. But why is it awkward? We all have genitals – it's the celebrated defining factor of our birth – and we all have sensations and urges (albeit varying), so why do we go the colour of beetroot and hide behind a cushion the minute someone starts to get fresh on the telly? Quite simply, it's learned behaviour.

My nan was the absolute worst person to watch anything with that didn't have a U rating. The *minute* someone on the telly started snogging or getting touchy-feely she would start vocalising it to cover up her own embarrassment: 'Oooh there they go. He looks like he's going to chew her face off!' Her commentary was considerably more cringe than the act taking place on the box in front of us, and I used to sink into the sofa and quietly die behind a cushion, praying that someone would switch the channel to spare us all.

My nan was certainly not unusual in her prudish and proper views, but instead of just going with it, not making it out to be weird, and instead normalising it as an important part of showing affection to a partner, I learned that sex was something to be awkward and embarrassed about.

Thankfully, I learned to duck out of the living room the moment Phil and Sharon were about to get it on over a car bonnet in *EastEnders* before I could be subjected to yet more of my nan's cringe commentary, and fortunately as my life has gone on it's a learned behaviour and opinion I have shaken off.

In some cultures – in the Amazon, for example – people happily mooch around naked. The human body is regarded as beautifully natural without anything required to be covered up, and boobs and willies are no more sniggered at or sexualised in day-to-day life than an arm or leg.

In Western society it's a bit different and that's OK too. I couldn't imagine jumping on the train to work butt-naked with my slightly sagging norks on show to Commuter-ville. More than anything, it'd be bloody cold! We don't live in a tropical jungle so we need clothes for practical reasons first and foremost, but we're also pretty reserved as a nation when it comes to sex and nudity. We have evolved to be rather prudish about our bits and mating – you only have to go to a safari park to see how other animal species give zero shits about having a bunk-up for all to see!

A lot of our attitudes come from our upbringing. Some families wouldn't dream of talking about topics such as sex and bodies (my grandmother), and others are a bit more laissez-faire about such matters. And to me that's great. Sex is about as natural as the basic concept of life gets. Without it none of us would be here.

My parents were fairly typically middle class in their values and stance on such matters. It wasn't banned or considered dirty or forbidden as a topic, but my folks were certainly embarrassed to talk about it. As my brothers and I navigated puberty little nuggets of information would be drip-fed to us instead, usually in literary form, by my ever-concerned and loving (and VERY British in their approach) folks. Did anyone else have the infamous book of the 1980s *The Body Book*? It had pride of place on our landing bookcase and was well thumbed by the three of us when we needed answers to the changes and feelings that suddenly took over our bodies.

Sex is the most basic and natural act of love we can express, and it's fundamental in a loving partnership. It's what separates a friendship from an intimate relationship.

However, sex is without a doubt one of the most contentious topics in relationships. It literally makes or breaks couples. It can be all-consuming and it can be incredibly complicated. It can be plentiful and it can be drier than the Sahara Desert. This chapter is all about leaving any awkwardness at the door, and being open and flexible about your thoughts, beliefs and behaviours around sex, in order to lead the most fulfilling and authentic relationship possible.

Oops, we have a problem

Let's get one thing straight. There is no such thing as a perfect sex life. Magazines, movies... they might portray glossy perfection when it comes to getting down and dirty, but even the most happy and committed couples can have blips in the bedroom. Life carries with it so many ups and downs, and it can have an effect on our sex life when we least expect or want it to. If you find yourself worried about your sex life, wondering if it's as healthy as it should be, then rest assured – you're definitely not alone.

First, let's ditch this word 'should'. It's such a bullshit word when it comes to heaping unnecessary pressure and stress on ourselves. 'We really *should* be having sex more.' 'I *should* make more of an effort,' 'He *should* be giving me more affection.' These are all sentences I've heard from disgruntled couples. But the very notion of the word 'should' is a negative one and serves no real positive reward, particularly when it comes to the intimate and sensitive matter of sex.

'Shoulds' are an active form of self-criticism, of measuring oneself against others, and they're steeped in a judgement that we aren't doing well enough. 'Should' statements are a common negative thinking pattern, which often only serves to bash our self-esteem and confidence, makes us feel guilty or as if we've failed, and puts unreasonable demands on ourselves. So before you flagellate yourself any more about what you or your partner 'should' be doing, let's take this utterly unhelpful word off the table and start focusing on what the situation actually is, and what you *could* do about it.

There are many fairly commonplace issues around sex, including stress, body hang-ups, past trauma, performance anxiety and a fear of intimacy. The most common challenges I hear about are:

- Differing sex drives
- Stuck in the same routine
- Lack of spontaneity

- Feeling disconnected from each other
- Too busy for sex
- Too tired! (mainly from parents with kids under the age of five)
- Being the one to always initiate
- Lack of foreplay
- Just not enough of it!

Few relationships are plain sailing, many have challenges around intimacy from time to time, and instead of brushing things under the carpet it's important to confront any issues and talk them through before resentment or disconnect kicks in.

I've seen too many couples avoid communicating with each other over their sex lives when things hit a rough patch, and in many cases it knocks self-esteem and becomes one of those awkward things, hanging in the air like a bad smell. Talking about sex is never quite as fun as the act itself, but a healthy and happy sex life thrives on open communication.

Less sex? More talking!

You're not alone if talking about sex is as appealing as cleaning out the cat litter tray. Many people are quite happy *doing* it, yet talking about it is a whole other thing. However, if things start to get a bit stale in the (making) love stakes, it's always useful to have that chat early doors to ensure whatever's going on (or not, as the case may be) doesn't become a bigger problem.

If you haven't talked openly about sex with your partner before, or it's a sensitive subject, it might feel embarrassing and awkward. These pointers can help the conversation kickstart and flow.

Keep the language positive: As we discussed in chapter 3, keep all tricky conversations in the first person and start with an 'I' sentence, as opposed to a 'you' one. 'I feel that we aren't having as much sex as we used to' is much less confrontational than 'You never put out any more.' It opens up the discussion instead of putting your partner on a defensive back foot.

Refer to the issue as a 'situation': Don't make it about something your partner has or hasn't done. For example, 'We haven't had sex or been intimate in a while' is much nicer and less judgemental than 'You haven't made any effort to have sex with me for ages.' It keeps the conversation on neutral ground where no one feels personally attacked or criticised – which is the ultimate passion killer!

Listen without interrupting: This can be a challenge for a lot of couples, but it's imperative that any issues are voiced with complete respect and you both have the space to do so. It may be difficult to articulate what you're feeling and, in turn, hard to hear what the other has to say, but an honest, open conversation is important in order to work out how you can get through the blip.

Put yourself in their shoes: One of the biggest gifts I can give you is the gift of perspective – in this instance, your partner's. Taking on board things from your partner's point of view will help massively in working out why your sex life is up for discussion and where their head is at. Things of such an intimate nature are not always obvious, even when you're in a relationship together, so being able to fully listen and respect what might be going on for your other half will help with rapport, understanding and empathy for each other.

Thank each other: It might sound a bit corny, but acknowledging and thanking each other for confronting a tricky topic will go a long way to reconnecting you both. Saying 'thank you' releases endorphins and the feel-good hormones dopamine and serotonin. This will put you in a good place mentally for working out how you move forwards.

“We used to have sex all the time. Now I’m lucky if we have it once a month. She’s just too tired from working and dealing with the kids.”

Dev, 37

Look who’s s***ging?

One of the most common issues with couples and sex is ‘Are we having enough of it?’ I only have to open up the question on my various WhatsApp groups (consisting of men *and* women) to hear a cacophony of ‘We just can’t be arsed’ and ‘I’m sure we aren’t having it enough.’ But what really constitutes ‘enough’? And whose standards are we measuring it against?

According to YouGov, over a quarter of the UK population are having sex at least once a week – 11% do it once, 7% have it twice and apparently 9% are getting jiggy three times a week! A third of Brits are sexually inactive and a similar number are having sex, but it’s been more than a week.

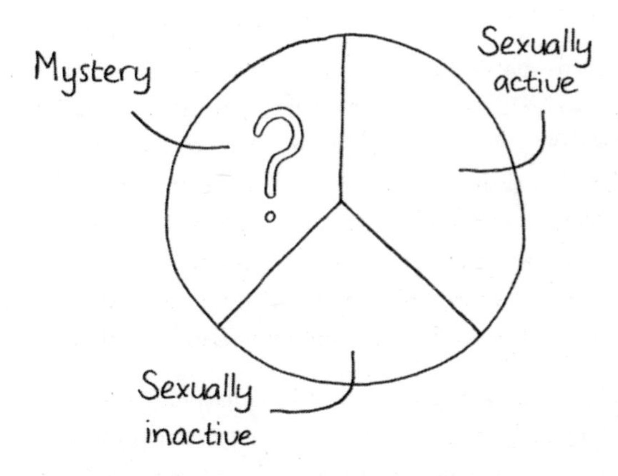

People in their late 20s are more likely to be having regular sex than any other age group and by the late 30s nearly two in five people aren’t having it regularly. Nearly a fifth of people in their 40s aren’t having sex at all and by the time we reach the mid-70s over half of the population are reporting as sexually inactive.

Now, I don't know about you, but I think these findings are pretty interesting, not least the great news that nearly half of golden oldies are still enjoying a decent sex life (major respect!), but the majority of the statistics don't particularly surprise me. I think it's pretty fair to assume that the younger you are the more frequently you're getting it on – the very fact that twentysomethings generally and biologically have more energy is reason enough.

However, the one finding that genuinely made me balk in disbelief was the fact that apparently one in four people are having sex *at least* once a week! Once a WEEK?! In fact, other reports suggest that it's even higher, with one in two people getting some action once a week. The reason I was slightly taken aback is that my own mini research, which consisted of polling friends, followers, clients, and anyone else who would willingly offer up such a personal admission, leads me to think that a 'couple of times a month' is far more realistic. Parents of kids under five years old tend to say even less than that, mainly due to feeling 'utterly knackered', with once every couple of months being a far more common answer.

The thing is, it really doesn't matter how often you're having sex. If you feel loved, happy and satisfied with your partner, then it's likely you're having the right amount of physical intimacy. Alternatively, if you're not feeling loved, happy or satisfied, it doesn't automatically mean that copious amounts of sex will solve it.

It's the quality of physical intimacy over the quantity of it that really counts in a relationship, and that you're both feeling loved and satisfied. And it goes so much deeper than just the act of having sex. One study I read suggests that 'positive behaviours' enhance how much good sex we're giving and receiving. In other words, the more generous, loving and thoughtful we are to our partner outside of the bedroom, the better the sex in quality *and* quantity.

I have a new client who can totally relate to this. She was getting increasingly frustrated with her husband over his laziness and tendency to have more than 'just one' in the pub, so that each time he tried it on with her she'd be feeling so cheesed off she just wasn't in the mood.

In fact, she resented being pestered for sex when she felt so utterly disregarded in the other areas of their relationship that she purposefully started rejecting him as 'punishment'.

However, as we know, tit for tat is a dangerous ol' game, and rarely works; it just breeds even more contempt. After a few coaching sessions they agreed to put the emphasis on what they did *outside* the bedroom to see what impact it might have on their intimacy levels.

He started being more proactive around the house and instead of popping to the local for a few bevvies would cook dinner with his wife and they would enjoy a bottle of wine together. It literally only took a couple of days and their sex life was reignited. It may sound so small and so simple, but it's often these subtle tweaks that can have the biggest impact and make a huge positive change. In this case, she was chuffed to bits at her husband's thoughtfulness and the fact they were spending more time together that she naturally warmed back up to him and wanted to show her love and appreciation – bingo, sex was back in the game and both felt much more fulfilled within the relationship.

So, the question of how much sex you should be having really is as unique and bespoke as your relationship. More fun and better communication outside as well as inside the bedroom will absolutely help in keeping intimacy ticking along nicely. Having sex once a week might be the average according to the various polls and reports, but what really matters is what works for *you* and *your partner*.

The benefits of having sex

When it comes to relationships, sex can sometimes get a bit of bad rap. After the initial excitement, sex can often be relegated to the sidelines – something that's not quite as regular or carefree as the earlier days, but instead regarded as time-consuming, knackering and a tad messy. 'Sex fatigue' as I've dubbed it is definitely a thing among couples. It's fair to assume that 'life' will affect your libido and it can happen to either party at any time. Stress, loss, mental health, physical problems – they can all have an impact on someone's attitude, interest and desire when it comes to a healthy sex life.

But let's be positive here, sex (as long as it's consensual and you're doing it with someone you fancy) is bloody fun and utterly enjoyable. There is no more intimate an act of expressing your love and/or attraction to someone than taking part in a jolly good bunk-up. There's no denying that sex not only feels great (most of the time), but – this might perk you up a smidge – it's also *good* for us. Yes, sex actually carries with it many health benefits.

So if things have been getting a bit stale and samey in the bedroom, fear not! We're going to perk that up during this chapter *and* embrace the added health and wellbeing benefits of how sex can give you so more than an orgasm.

Here's what else regular sex can do for you:

It's anti-ageing! According to research by clinical neuroscientist Dr David Weeks, older men and women who have an active sex life look five to seven years younger than their actual age. And he cites 'quality over quantity' as important in achieving these anti-ageing benefits. Essentially, if the sex is loving, it's being reflected in our glowing youthful skin.

Is great for the immune system: Sexually active people take fewer sick days says sexual health expert and PhD Yvonne K Fullbright. This is because people who have sex have a higher level of an antibody which fights germs and viruses.

(One for the mums here) Boosts pelvic floor and improves bladder control: It may or may not surprise you to know that 30% of women have weak pelvic floor muscles (I'm a fully signed-up member of that club, FYI), which can lead to bladder incontinence. Having sex, and more importantly an orgasm, causes the muscles to contract, which helps strengthen them.

Burns calories: If you're struggling to summon the motivation to go the gym, then perhaps consider some 'home exercise' instead. Sex uses around 5 calories a minute, so if you fancy working off that cheeky donut, have a half-hour sex sesh and you're quits. A donut *and* an orgasm – I'd say that's a win-win.

Raises confidence: Having good sex is widely regarded as a confidence booster. When we have sex we feel good – simple. People who are sexually active are reported to feel more confident about their bodies and appearance too.

Is a mood booster: We all know that exercise is good for our mental health and that's because when our heart rate is raised the brain's natural feel-good chemical, serotonin (the happy hormone), is released. The same thing happens when we have sex – serotonin floods our body making us feel happy and relaxed.

Is a stress buster: It's not only our mood that improves when we make love. Our stress levels are much more manageable in the 24-hour period after having sex. Cortisol, which is the hormone responsible for making us feel stressed, reduces when we enjoy those post-coital cuddles.

Creates more sex: Like many things in life, say the gym, if you're out of practice you start to forget what it's like, why you should bother and what to do – motivation soon wanes. Sex is the same, so the best way to boost your libido is to 'get back on the horse' so to speak. The more you have sex, the more you'll be inclined to want it.

Improves sleep: It's quite common to want to nod off the moment you've climaxed – and for good reason. After an orgasm the hormone prolactin, which is responsible for making you feel relaxed and sleepy, is released. So if you're needing a sleep aid, why not have an orgasm at the same time, eh?

Reduces pain: Cue all the jokes about 'Not tonight darlin' I've got a headache.' Well, actually there's no need to take a couple of painkillers, just have some nookie. Due to the love hormone oxytocin and a whole bunch of other brain chemicals being released during sex, it acts as a natural form of pain relief. Women find period cramps can ease after having an orgasm, and pain reduction in headaches and arthritis has also been widely reported.

Wards off prostate cancer: A fascinating and awesome fact this one: having sex is said to help stave off prostate cancer! Research suggests that men who ejaculate regularly are less likely to get prostate cancer due to the prostate being cleared of toxins, which could otherwise linger and cause cancerous changes.

Puts a spring in your step: Fan of a morning bunk-up? If not you might want to reconsider putting some effort into a little 'top of the morning' sexy time. People who have some morning loving report feeling upbeat for the rest of the day. Forget the coffee, copulate instead.

> “There is nothing that puts me in a good mood and makes me feel more confident and sexy than having good sex with my boyfriend.”
>
> Pani, 29

Can't touch this

According to a report from relationship support charity Relate and YouGov, most people say that sexuality and intimate relationships are important to their identity and sense of wellbeing, and a healthy sex life is a significant goal and expectation in a good relationship. So, if sex is an important part of our general wellbeing, it stands to reason that if issues and challenges crop up we're going to feel less happy and satisfied with life, too.

Sex can also put enormous pressure on a relationship. Counsellors and therapists often see couples who are struggling, where sexual problems are causing a strain, and when sexual dissatisfaction is prevalent it can reduce overall relationship satisfaction. Sex shouldn't be, and isn't, the be all and end all of being in a happy and healthy twosome, but it's certainly something which is important to many, and should be treated with sensitivity and respect, especially if all is not well.

The most recent poll from Relate's *Let's Talk About Sex* report suggests that only a third of people are satisfied with their sex lives. Men are more likely to be lacking in satisfaction than women, and the most dissatisfied age group are people in their 20s. People who identify as gay, lesbian, bisexual or other are reported to be slightly less satisfied with their sex lives than those in heterosexual relationships.

So what's going on? Why might we be feeling a bit 'meh' when it comes to our sex lives and our libido? There are several reasons why any of us might sometimes feel about as 'up for it' as we are for a dog food sandwich, and it's important we recognise and talk about any challenges, worries and issues as soon as they emerge to keep our relationships ticking along and tended to.

I had a client who enjoyed, in his words, 'a pretty decent sex life'. Attractive to the ladies with a killer smile and self-deprecating confidence, he'd certainly never struggled for attention. However, he came to me for help having experienced a sudden decline in his libido. He was in a fairly new relationship, which was going well. However, with the initial honeymoon phase over, when it came to having sex he had started to make excuses and avoid it.

This troubled him. He was very attracted to his girlfriend. He'd never had issues in the past and yet every time she instigated sex he described something similar to getting the ick (see chapter 2 for more on that). He basically didn't want it any more and would do anything to avoid it, *but* he still fancied her. It was really confusing him.

After a good chat and mental unpack, we uncovered various stresses and concerns he had been ruminating over on a much more subconscious level. Worries over a past relationship and financial 'baggage' that had cropped up plus a concern over being able to provide for his new lady should the relationship turn into something more official were affecting his mood and stress levels without him really realising. Feeling worried and overthinking a hypothetical situation, as he was, can absolutely be enough to upset the apple cart when it comes to matters of a more delicate nature, i.e. his sex drive and desire.

Working out what was going on in his head and vocalising those niggles helped him realise how connected our mental health is to our physical health, and that he wasn't some sort of sex robot who could turn it on whenever it was required. I congratulated him on seeking help and he was relieved to realise the trigger for his sudden decrease in sexual appetite actually had a very valid reason: he was in a right old tizz about an ex and finances, and stress + sexual urges = computer says no.

Thankfully, good old communication saved the day and after letting his lady friend in on what was troubling him he felt a million times better. And by association she did too. She had been getting more and more concerned, and as the sexy-time evasiveness had started to creep out of control was wondering 'Is it me?' Once she knew what was going on, her self-doubt turned into empathy, and it had a happy ending (excuse the pun). After working through his past relationship issues, their own relationship went on in leaps and bounds.

It can be incredibly hard to confront problems when it comes to sex. It's just so utterly personal and when it involves another person it can be embarrassing, and a perceived threat to our masculinity or femininity. But let me tell you right here, right now, sexual problems can affect anyone at any time, regardless of age, sexual preferences or experiences. In fact, one in three of us have experienced a sexual problem, so you're definitely not alone if you have too.

Sexual problems are more common than you may realise. According to the Relate's *Let's Talk About Sex* report mentioned on page 144, half a million Brits are diagnosed each year with an STI, only a third of people overall are satisfied with their sex lives, and nearly one in five of the population have a differing sex drive to their partner, which puts a strain on a relationship.

So let's talk about sex, what might be causing the wrong kind of bump in the night and how to improve it.

Loss of libido

Many people experience a decreased sex drive from time to time. Life happens and it stands to reason that there will be times when the thought of getting fresh and frisky leaves you feeling as cold as the bed sheets. There are many reasons for a loss of libido and they can include:

Mental health: Depression, anxiety, stress, low mood, trauma... all can have a big effect on your desire for sex. Lack of interest in activities is a big symptom of depressive disorders and that can include sex. Medication such as antidepressants can also cause side effects, which may include a loss of sex drive.

What to do about it: Talking therapies can be hugely effective in working through negative or troubling thoughts, feelings and behaviours. Meditation, mindfulness, yoga and hypnotherapy are all useful alternative therapies to try to aid self-awareness and relaxation. If you're on medication your doctor might be able to recommend something else that doesn't affect your libido as negatively.

'Performance issues': Erectile dysfunction (impotence) and premature ejaculation can be concerning for the man experiencing it. It can happen for a number of reasons, including past trauma, physical or emotional problems, feeling pressure to perform, stress, anxiety, tiredness, diabetes, hormone disorders, too much alcohol or drugs. The same can apply for women (minus the erection concern), but pregnancy, post-birth complications, perimenopause and menopause, and body confidence can all affect sexual desire, too.

What to do about it: Feeling or being unable to physically have sex can be extremely distressing. And it's a vicious cycle: the more we stress about it, the less likely we'll be jumping into action when we want to. Seeking help from a medical professional such as a sex therapist (one offering psychosexual therapy) can help to explore and overcome sexual dysfunctions. Your GP may be able to investigate any of the more physical concerns, and couples counselling can be highly effective in helping a couple address and confront the stalemate situation. Feeling more understood and taking any 'blaming' off the table can encourage relaxation and help overcome performance issues in the bedroom.

Pain during sex: They say pleasure and pain can be closely linked – it certainly worked for Ana and Christian Grey in *Fifty Shades* – but anyone who has experienced a searing toothache while biting into an ice cream will tell you it's an experience to be avoided at all costs. You can quite understand, then, that if you experience any sort of unpleasant pain during sex, it's not going to make you want to repeat the experience – your ability to be turned *on* will very much be turned *off* the minute said deed is even mooted. Pain or discomfort during or after sex shouldn't be ignored. It could be a sign of an infection or illness, or a physical or psychological problem. Vaginal dryness in women as a result of hormonal changes can be common, and can cause severe discomfort and/or pain during intercourse. For men, pain during sex (dyspareunia), can occur during and after ejaculation.

What to do about it: First, don't leave it! Feeling pain during and after sex is not fun and you should be seen to by a medical professional. Seek advice from your GP or a sexual health clinic. For ladies experiencing vaginal dryness, over-the-counter lubricants are available for both men and women, which can be a great help, and you may want to see a doctor. Alternative therapies such as hypnotherapy can be useful to challenge and manage any feelings of pain, and reframe it in a different, more manageable way.

Different (sex) drives: Many couples report an imbalance of libido at some point in their relationship. Perhaps one wants it more than the other, maybe boredom between the sheets has seeped in. Having different sex drives can cause feelings of guilt because you're not satisfying your partner or perhaps a worry of no longer being attractive to your other half. As we know, there can be so many reasons for loss of libido, but when it becomes unbalanced between a couple it needs addressing before misunderstandings occur or frustrations surface.

What to do about it: An honest and open conversation about this is key. It may be awkward to talk about, but anything unbalanced which could cause conflict needs addressing and discussing fairly. What can change and what can't change? Is there a compromise that can be reached, so both feel sexually satisfied but without pressure from the other? It might not sound very sexy, but compromise and negotiation are important with all elements of a relationship, and that includes your sex life. Ask each other how important it is? What would you ideally both like and when? And what does it give you (apart from the obvious gratification), i.e. closeness, stability, love? Have a think about spicing things up in the bedroom, perhaps take some inspiration from outside sources and try some new positions, introduce some sex toys, watch some pornography together or have a little dabble with some role play. Whatever you *both* feel comfortable doing together may help give that libido a little boost.

> “I struggled with being able to 'get it up' for years after having an adult circumcision due to medical reasons. Every time I went to have sex all I could think of was 'Is it going to hurt?' My girlfriend was really understanding and after getting some help from a counsellor and the doctor, I'm finally able to enjoy a good sex life. We're BOTH grateful!”
>
> Adam, 26

Let's get it on...

If you've been shoving sex down the list of priorities along with the never ending ironing pile, it's time to reframe how you position (no pun intended) the importance of sex and intimacy in your relationship, and what they give you both. Remember, if you're both happy and satisfied with the amount of sex you are, or aren't, having then that is right for you. Keep communicating to check you're both feeling satisfied and, if not, work together on ways to ensure each other feels loved and physically wanted.

It's not just about sex, it's about emotional and physical intimacy. Anyone can engage in a meaningless quickie, so let's shake things up a bit, take the pressure off and try taking sex off the table. Explore *other* ways to intimately connect. This is a great activity for those struggling with libido and tiredness issues.

We're going to have a play with a bit of reverse psychology. If someone says you *can't* have something, your desire and fixation on that thing kicks in. Let's take a cream cake. If I'm on a diet and someone tells me I can't have that cream cake, all I'll want is that sodding cream cake. Even if I don't really want it, the very notion of being told I can't have it will propel me into wanting it and pestering the person to give it to me.

Now let's take this notion with sex in a couple. If partner 1 is chomping at the bit, pestering for some action, and the other is totally exhausted and stressed with work, and saying no, the mismatch is likely to cause frustration and friction. Partner 1 will just become fixated on having sex and increasingly aggravated when it's denied, and partner 2 will feel increasingly guilty, pressured and even less likely to want to engage in it.

So here's where we flip things.

- Agree to have a chat about your sex life, and calmly and respectfully say what the situation feels like from your point of view. Remember to avoid using 'You never' or 'You don't' statements so you don't push each other further away. Use 'I feel,' 'I would like' or 'It would mean XYZ to me if...' statements to keep things well communicated and neutral.

- Agree some time together where sex is *not* part of the plan. Take it off the pedestal and put it to one side for now. Instead, it's going to be all about exploring each other, enjoying each other and being with each other intimately without sex being the end goal. There is no ulterior motive other than just appreciating each other physically.
- Start by hugging. Cuddling reduces stress and increases bonding between a couple. Hold each other's gaze. It might feel a bit awkward, but holding eye contact with each other can build trust, intimacy and passion. Don't make it all weird, like some hypnotherapy stare-off, but simply sitting or lying opposite each other and looking into each other's eyes helps to reconnect.
- Kiss! OK, many of us may have not snogged like a hormonal teen at a disco for yonks, but kissing is really sexy. Many couples admit they don't bother to kiss much any more, but couples who kiss more frequently report higher levels of relationship satisfaction. Have a peck on the lips, perhaps go in for the full 'pash', but also explore other areas to kiss your partner (hands, neck, shoulders) to enjoy intimacy.
- Get touchy-feely. Show one another appreciation by intimately touching. Perhaps a massage, stroking each other naked, licking, perhaps some gentle foreplay... without any expectation or promise of sex. Often just touching and enjoying each other's bodies is rushed or disregarded completely in sex, which for the one 'not up for it' is like being expected to smash a 100-metre sprint with no warm-up – in other words, it's challenging.

Now here's the beauty of this exercise: with the pressure and expectation removed from the start, i.e. 'We don't have to have sex', what you might find naturally happening is the very thing you're not expecting – sex.

> Partner 1 hasn't been told they 'can't' so feels satisfied with the intimacy and partner 2 feels less pressured and harassed to 'wham bam thankyou mam'. Instead, both are on a level playing field, both are enjoying the intimacy and effort, and what might naturally take place as a result is the icing on the cake. The key is not putting sex as a goal for this exercise. The point of it is really *not* to have sex, but to enjoy each other in other ways to boost your emotional and physical intimacy.

Fertility and conception sex!

'Let's make a baby darling...' The words will either spark giddy joy or utter terror depending on where you are in the baby-making journey. I can say from personal experience that there is nothing more unfun or unsexy as conception sex.

It often starts out with a lot of excitement, hope and anticipation, and, if you're one of the fortunate ones who hit the jackpot pretty quickly, it's a job well done and John Lewis baby section here we come. But if, as for many others, the decision and then the subsequent trying for a baby is much less straightforward, it can be a major source of stress and seriously testing for even the most robust relationships.

According to the NHS, around one in seven couples will have difficulty conceiving. Fertility issues can affect anyone at any time and for many reasons. Age has an effect on the likelihood of conceiving naturally, mainly for women, as well conditions like endometriosis, ovulation issues such as polycystic ovary syndrome (PCOS), and in men low sperm count. There are, however, many other reasons why a couple has issues getting pregnant and if you've been trying unsuccessfully for over a year (six months if over 35) it's recommended to seek medical advice to get to the bottom of it.

Fertility and trying to conceive (TTC) without a doubt puts an enormous strain on a relationship. Many couples going through the process of fertility treatment report that the psychological strain is much worse than the physical side of the treatment. And what was once a pleasurable act, i.e. sex, often becomes an emotionally loaded and fraught duty, which can be hard to grapple with.

I have witnessed first-hand the exasperation of a colleague being summoned home instantly to 'do the deed' as his wife announced via text that she was ovulating. The poor chap was halfway through his lunch when he grabbed his coat and darted off to do his part. I could just imagine his lovely lady lying there, legs akimbo, ready for the money shot! Who said romance is dead, eh? But even though I jest, trying to get pregnant can be bloody hard and the impact it can have on a couple's relationship and sex life is too huge to ignore.

Trying to conceive can create conflict and tension, but it can also bring couples closer together, so recognise the challenges and work together to hopefully get the outcome you're both after.

It's in the timing: Couples trying to time having sex to get pregnant experience greater sexual dysfunction. Try to enjoy sex at other times of the month too, not just when it's the baby-making window. It'll help to take the spotlight off it and allow you to enjoy the act of sex without pressure.

Team work: Agree who you are/aren't going to tell about your fertility journey. It's a highly personal thing for any couple and can be a very sensitive subject. Many couples choose to keep such topics private and not for the family WhatsApp gossip. Work together as a team to ensure only the people you really want to share such news with are in on it.

Avoid the blame game: It's common for one or both of the couple to feel guilty about being the 'one with the issue', leading to fears that the other one will leave. Self-blame is quite common too in an attempt to take the emotional burden away from the other person, but it's rarely helpful. Talk to your partner about your fears and keep reassuring each other.

Competitive victim mode: Who has got it worse? Is it her who has had umpteen invasive procedures? Or him who's been subjected to a sperm-collecting posh wank in a doctor's waiting room? Feeling hard done by and 'I've had it worse' can lead to bitterness and resentment. Remove any tit for tat from the equation and take a moment to respect what each other is going through with no judgement.

The future? TTC and fertility treatment can be a long road for many. It can also be extremely expensive. Having open honest chats about your financial situation, your options, other plans and next steps will help you to keep moving forwards, even if one teeny step at a time.

Take a moment

Sex can be a tricky old game. Feelings, desires, intentions, hopes, dreams, needs, emotions… there's just so much that goes into it. When things get overwhelming or stuck in a rut, it can be helpful to take a pause, and view your feelings and what's going on from a different perspective in the hope it makes better sense of the whole situation. This exercise is to do by yourself. You will take on the 'role' of each of the viewpoints as you change chairs.

- Put two chairs out in the room. Make sure chair 2 is at a distance from chair 1. Chair 1 is your point of view, chair 2 is the 'observer'.
- Sit in chair 1, facing chair 2 and think about how you're feeling. Vocalise any worries, thoughts or feelings and allow yourself to fully offload into the room.
- Next go and sit in chair 2, facing chair 1. From this position imagine you're viewing you in chair 1 from a few moments before. What do you notice? What are you experiencing, thinking, feeling looking at and hearing from this 'you'? What advice would you give 'you' in chair 1?
- Shake yourself off and return to your position in chair 1. How do you feel now? Has anything changed?

This can be a great exercise to let out any frustrations or worries, and a chance to gain perspective from the other viewpoint to help things feel more agreeable.

It's complicated

Sex is such a natural thing and should be enjoyed by anyone who wants to partake of it, but there are also other kinds of sexual activities, ranging from casual 'non-committal' sex and friends with benefits (sometime referred to as f**k buddies) to masturbation and the use of pornography, either solo or with a partner. These can be positive or negative things depending on what's going on for the individual at the time.

The majority of relationships are monogamous (one partner at a time), but there are plenty of people who don't subscribe to exclusivity and who value enjoying more than one partner. At the present time, polyamory (or having more than one sexual partner at once) seems to be having a moment, with more and more people seeking the benefits of having one's cake and eating it (polyamory is not to be confused with polygamy or marrying multiple spouses, which is effectively illegal in the UK). However, as liberating and fulfilling as having multiple partners can be, it should still be considered with caution.

Having more than one intimate partner can create issues should any one party start to get more involved than has been agreed. Feelings can and often do develop, even if that wasn't the original intention. The very nature of having sex and being intimate fires up all the feel-good hormones responsible for attachment, bonding and love, and due to the sharing of partners, jealously can also be a very real challenge.

So unless you are absolutely sure you can handle the possible repercussions of what being in an open relationship might be like, proceed with care. Whatever your situation, remember to go with the flow, look after yourself, be safe, communicate with whoever you need to, and remind yourself that you deserve a happy and fulfilled sex life.

7

KNOWING ME, KNOWING YOU

Bring it on home to me

Even the strongest relationships need work. Relationships evolve, we evolve, and it's all about recognising when you need extra vigilance to help keep things ticking along like a well-oiled machine.

This chapter is all about future-proofing your relationship. It is also about *you*. You can never be the best to anybody else until you are the best to yourself, and that's something I stand by to help maintain good emotional and mental wellbeing. It's pretty obvious, isn't it. If you run yourself ragged, aren't true to your feelings and aren't prioritising yourself, then how can you be a great partner? A healthy happy relationship starts with you.

I have many clients who come to me seeking help with their relationship challenges – and there is almost always an imbalance of self-care. Sometimes couples have lost sight of enjoying activities *outside* the relationship which can enrich them, boost self-confidence and self-esteem, and inject positive energy into the relationship. Other couples spend too much time apart and separate from their relationships. A balance is key – and we're going to explore that in this chapter.

Whatever stage you might be at, it's about building on the foundations of not only you, but also your partnership. Anyone who thinks that they have done enough and have ticked all the boxes on their relationship needs to wake up and smell the coffee!

There's no room for complacency – relationships are constantly evolving; variables and influences (such as work changes and intervening friendships) test us frequently, so we must always be alert and on the ball to ensure we're content and moving forwards. A relationship stuck in a rut, that is stagnant, is no fun for anyone.

Let's imagine your relationship is the plans for a swanky new apartment block – you know, one of those sexy ones on the river Thames. From the moment your relationship starts to grow wings and dating starts to have a little slap and tickle with 'commitment', imagine this is the start of the foundation work of what hopefully will become a tall, magnificent, robust apartment block – unshakeable, standing proud and admired by others.

As you reach each new stage with your partner, perhaps getting over your first argument, deciding to move in together, buying a dog, signing up to peloton, having kids, envisage each of these important affirming moments as new levels added to your relationship tower.

The tower can go as high as it can go and at all times you need to keep aiming for the penthouse (whatever that might mean to you). It needs to be just in reach at all times and you should continue to keep striving to reach it, but you never want to get there, get too comfy and not be able to maintain it. Thinking this way keeps the motivation, energy and focus on your relationship, and you both actively engaged.

So how are we going to keep that focus and energy on 'us'? How can we make sure we're prioritising ourselves and each other? Finding your way and your rhythm takes time, an open mind and being prepared to adapt as your relationship evolves over time.

We know how important communication is within a couple. It's something we all should do, but it's perfectly understandable that we fall a bit short sometimes. Life is busy – work, friends, family and hobbies dominate our diaries and all too often it's our relationships that come crashing down around our ears and suffer in the wake of not being prioritised. At best it's being knackered, at worst it's falling out of love. No one wants to feel taken for granted, sidelined or, even worse, ignored, so let's do all we can to make sure we're putting our love life at the top of our to-do list.

I believe in you

The strongest relationships are built on shared values and beliefs. We've explored this in chapter 1, where there are some helpful activities you might like to try to explore, identify and hone. Values are so important. They represent who we are, what makes us tick and what's important to us. Values drive what we do, how we think and how we feel. Beliefs are closely linked to values, their BFFs if you will, but they are based on experience and come about as a result of what you learn as you go through life.

Think of your values and beliefs as your core foundations. If you were in a values and beliefs X-ray machine, everything you stand for, what would be there? Take away all material possessions and whether you're tall or short, big or small, wearing Primark's finest or Chanel sliders, none of that matters. It's about who you are at your very core that drives everything you do in life. It's essentially why you exist, why you do what you do, and this is why it's so important in relationships.

Without definite values and beliefs it's very easy to start wafting around in the wind like a fart in a colander. Whenever I get a troubled client come to me with personal and relationship issues, feeling in a rut or unsure of where their life is heading, it's almost always because they have forgotten to tap into their values and the beliefs associated with them.

They feel destabilised, unsure of where they are heading, and almost certainly experiencing self-esteem and self-confidence issues. If you're not feeling sure of who you are, then it stands to reason you will be unsure of where your personal relationships are at. Blind leading the blind, right?!

Tuning back in to who you are and what your values are in life will go a long way towards creating your own inner peace, satisfaction and drive. The next step is *shared* values and beliefs with your partner and establishing a shared goal. It will undoubtedly help your relationship stand the test of time.

So how do we get there? How do we anchor those roots back in the ground? Try this next love hack to help you keep in tune not only with yourself, but each other.

Share as a pair

Tapping into each other's value and belief system will help keep you in tune with each other. It might feel a bit odd to just suddenly enquire about your other half's 'values and beliefs', so instead word values and beliefs in a way that feels accessible and normal to you. In the words of *The Greatest Showman* classic, I like to define it as 'This is me!' If it helps, sing the actual song as you're tuning into your values – no one's judging! Essentially, it's about teasing out what 'rules' you live your life by.

- Do this as a couple. Each write down your values. You might find it easier to just underline items on the list I've borrowed from the internet, which you'll find on page 177.
- Try to identify around 10 to 20 core values each. Next re-read them and whittle them down to your top five. This might seem hard, but you'll find that some values naturally go with others, i.e. truth and honesty, so allow groups to form, then figure out the overall value of that group. For example, if you've picked truth, honesty, authenticity, fairness, communication and humility, they're all connected, so the overall value here might be fairness. You value fairness the most out of all the similar values, so this is a top value.

- When you've got five, order them from one to five, and for each of those write down a belief that is attached to that value. Remember, a belief is why you know that value to be true and important to you. For example, fairness = a belief I hold around fairness is that everyone should be treated with respect and as an individual.
- Write it as a statement: 'I value XXXXX because XXXXX' or 'I value fairness because I believe everyone should be treated with respect and as an individual.'
- *Other examples are:* 'I value honesty because it helps with gaining trust and nurturing a healthy transparent relationship' or 'I value family because it gives me stability and allows me to be myself' or 'I value loyalty because it helps me to trust and be trusted in turn.'
- Now share your top five values and beliefs list with your partner. Look for the overlaps between you both, and embrace and explore any matches together. Any values and beliefs that don't match are fine, but it's really important to look at those ones too, recognise any feelings you each might have that *don't* align and consider what that might mean. Conflicting values and beliefs are not impossible to work with in a relationship, but it will take some understanding, communication and compromise to ensure they don't become an issue in your partnership.

Examples of values and conflicting beliefs might be:

- Value = wealth
- Conflicting beliefs = one partner might believe in earning money for themselves in order to support a lavish lifestyle, while the other partner might believe in living more modestly and giving to charity.
- Value = fairness
- Conflicting beliefs = one partner might believe that women should get six months of fully paid maternity leave, while the other partner might believe employers should not be required to pay their employees for this time off.

Actively taking the time to do this activity will help in two ways: first, you'll become surer of who you are and, second, you'll be more tuned into each other within your relationship, especially as things evolve, adapt and change.

One thing's for sure: as life motors on, things do and will change, and we need to be ready for that. Financial and job changes, loss and bereavement, health situations, new friends, hobbies and interests, having kids – all can affect us and our relationship to varying degrees. We're all on our own 'journey' and we need to keep mindful at all times of whoever is on it with us.

Look for the common ground. This will help remind you of why you're a great match, so discuss and work through any conflicting values and beliefs to find, at the very least, a middle ground of understanding.

> "We'd been married for 11 years and I realised that I had no clue what he wanted from life any more – and neither did I. Kids, work, moving house had all had an impact on 'us'. We needed a massive kick up the backside to remember why we were married and to get us back to being a happy couple again."
>
> Tracey, 41

Are you interested?

A common problem when relationships move from the honeymoon to the established partnership phase is that interests change. Perhaps you initially clicked over a shared passion for something, had a mutual love for a particular hobby or found a particular interest extremely attractive in your partner. Fast forward umpteen years and lolling around on the sofa, scratching one's undercarriage and getting a takeaway curry now constitutes having 'a passion for the culinary arts'.

So many couples lose their way when it comes to shared interests. Lots of them confide in me that they're completely baffled and lost as to why the relationship has lasted so long when they fail to share anything they once did.

There are a lot of factors at play here. First, we have to give ourselves a break and be kind. We're only human and life piles on a lot. Life is busy. Chuck into the mix having kids (you can put your hobbies on ice for quite some while with that one!), financial pressures, work commitments, friends and family demands, and you can see where the passion and uncomplicated fun you may have blissfully bonded over has gone.

If you're currently in a relationship, cast your mind back to when you first met your partner. Where did you meet and what were you doing? What did you first notice about them? What attracted you? How did they make you feel? Those first few dates, what did you talk about and bond over enough to want to take it on to the next level? Chances are you have piqued each other's interest due to shared values and joint interests. We may grow up and evolve, and we should, but it's how we evolve alongside our partner that ensures the relationship stays on course.

Change does happen, though. It may be a bit of a breakup cliché, but some people *do* change, and when you think about it, on balance that's not an unreasonable notion. Darren and Claire (not their real names) met in their local pub in their teens and have been together for 12 years. Just because Darren still wants to sink eight pints in the pub on a Friday night followed by a kebab chaser as his younger self once did, it doesn't mean that his missus Claire is being out of order because she's now over that particular pastime and prefers a more intimate social life.

Her interests have changed, his haven't. There is nothing wrong with either of their paths, until it starts to drive a wedge between a couple and the ol' blame game wafts in like a slow-release stink bomb. This is where some healthy compromise needs to arrive to clear the air.

Shared interests form part of your foundations. They create natural conversation, bonding over a shared passion and they help a couple feel closer. Hobbies can also be a great vehicle for carving out time to spend together – and I mean proper, meaningful, fulfilling time. Doing the Sainsbury's shop together once a week is *not* quality time; playing a game of tennis is. Taking a joint visit to the local dump is not quality time (fundamental yes, but quality it is not); cooking dinner together with a glass of vino and some tunes on is.

Take some time to take stock of what you used to like doing and what you'd like to do together now. Perhaps you haven't even thought about it for years! Individual interests are equally important, but let's focus on the interests that you can enjoy together.

Work together on your relationship to keep it fresh, alive and interesting. Be a role model for your mates, kids and colleagues, and instead of moaning about what you don't do any more, physically and mentally climb out of that clichéd trench and show by example how fulfilling your relationship is.

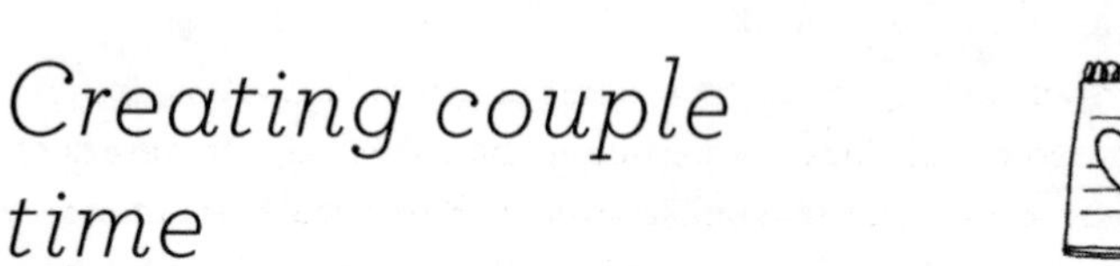

Creating couple time

We've spent time in this book looking at the romantic side of being in a couple, but the other super-important aspect to a relationship is friendship. Actually liking each other and wanting to spend time in your partner's company – wow, remember that! ☺

This activity is about reconnecting with your other half, setting time aside for each other and diarising it as 'high importance'. After all, what's more important than the person who's supposed to have your back – for better, for worse.

- Take a piece of paper each and draw a spidergram. In the middle write 'My interests' and then brainstorm everything you like and are interested in.
- When you're both done, share and compare your findings. If there are any common interests written down make a note of them.
- Now on a separate piece of paper draw another spidergram. This time, in the middle write 'Our interests'.

- Brainstorm together any joint interests that have come up on the individual diagrams and chat together to come up with new ideas which you both might like to try too. For example, cooking, baking, wine tasting, tennis club, home improvement, cycling, massage, walking, reading, photography, movie club, gardening, exercise, singing clubs etc.
- Agree on one new activity/hobby/interest that you'd *both* like to do and actively go about making a definite plan to action it.
- Plan ahead, and book a date and time in your joint calendars. Stick it on a wall planner, put a Post-it on the door, whatever works for you, and enjoy carving out that dedicated time for 'us time'.
- You may choose to sign up to a course or pay for something in advance so you can't easily flake or opt out. This helps if there is a tendency to get flaky. Make that verbal and physical commitment to show up to each other – I mean literally say it to each other – and enjoy prioritising your partnership while doing something you're both getting fulfilment from.
- You may choose to go one step further. On your original individual list, pick an interest that is different to your partner's and take turns each month, or whenever feels right, to introduce something new to each other.

“After the kids started school I suddenly realised I didn't do anything for me any more. We were both feeling a bit lost and when my partner said we didn't have any hobbies any more it was the wake-up call we needed. Every Thursday night we play at the local squash club as a doubles team and make full use of the babysitter with a pub dinner after – it's been a marriage game-changer!”

Lacey, 40

Interdependence

We now know the importance of spending quality, meaningful time together, but we've also touched on the fact that spending time separately is equally important. This is particularly key in a happy, well-rounded relationship. It's called interdependence.

You've probably heard of being *independent* and that can indeed be a great quality to have. Somebody who is independent is self-sufficient and self-reliant, and knows what makes them feel safe and secure. And then there's also the opposite of independent, which is *co-dependent.*

Co-dependency is a relationship which operates in a bit of a push-pull cycle. One person needs the other, probably more than the other person needs them back. But on the other hand the other person likes the feeling of being wanted and responsible for someone else, and probably needs to be needed.

This type of relationship can be tricky and often unhealthy, as a person who is in a co-dependent relationship often has trouble communicating their own thoughts and feelings, and instead seeks acceptance or finds their self-worth in taking on those of their partner.

Co-dependency signs to watch out for include your life revolving around your partner, either of you suffering from low self-esteem, making excuses for your partner's behaviour, or always feeling anxious or drained. You might constantly take on the role of rescuer or be an enabler, particularly where alcohol or drug abuse or money issues are concerned.

If you recognise any of these in your relationship then, first, be honest with yourself and your partner about what's going on, recognise your choices (you always have a choice) and be firm about making a change.

Being fully independent, or on the flip side, co-dependent, is not going to create a mutually healthy romantic relationship. As with most things in life, we need to find a more agreeable middle ground. We need to create connection, intimacy, respect and boundaries, and it's building an *interdependent* relationship that will give you the space to grow, while being authentic and fully yourself.

An interdependent relationship embraces and recognises the importance of time together, but also prioritises enjoying time outside the couple as well. Being interdependent allows you to support your other half whilst also focusing on your own personal growth, and vice versa.

You will achieve more success and happiness when you're connected to your partner, and when you also value your sense of self. It allows you both to be yourselves without any need to compromise on who you are or your value systems. It's the golden rule to relationship success and it's one of the main things I encourage couples to work on when there is an imbalance of power, control or neediness.

Hold on to the connection

Connection is what is important when it comes to being interdependent. Without connection it's hard to create intimacy with our partner. In fact, I would go on to say it's impossible if there is zilch connection between you. Any long-term relationship needs our emotional connection with each other to grow and develop.

Here are some other things to consider in order to maintain a kick-ass interdependent relationship:

Healthy boundaries: We know from previous chapters how important it is to set boundaries at the beginning of a relationship. They help create a framework and lines of respect for each other, which is massively important! One example might be respect for privacy, i.e. 'I'm comfortable sharing my house keys, car and my bed (!) with you, but looking through my phone or emails uninvited is not OK.'

Active listening: We also know how important communication is, and a huge part of this is carefully listening to each other and paying attention to what each other has to say. Tuning into your partner's tone and engaging with what they are trying to say will help you in knowing how to best respond too.

Your own interests: These allow for personal growth outside the relationship and they're really important. If you don't have them it doesn't mean you aren't committed to each other, but they demonstrate a healthy amount of independence. Sex aside, imagine how boring (and annoying) it would be to do the same thing, all the time, with the same person!

A big part of relationships is being able to take responsibility for your own actions or behaviours, instead of palming the blame off on your partner. This is a key part in an interdependent relationship, it can be a really tough one for couples as it requires ego to be left at the door and vulnerability to be invited in. One of the most empowering things we can do for ourselves, and our partner, is to admit when we are wrong and hold up our hands, taking responsibility for our part in the [interdependent] relationship.

Establishing and continuing to build an interdependent relationship will improve your self-esteem and self-confidence, things which are typically lacking in a co-dependent relationship, and often in a very independent one. This is because the partners in an apparently very independent couple may have lots of confidence on the surface, but the defensive walls are so far 'up' that they need to be lowered to a healthier level.

Always a work in progress

Encourage each other to adopt these healthy habits and keep working on yourselves patiently, helping each other build in time and space for that to be actioned without guilt. My husband and I make a real point of giving each other dedicated time to do something for ourselves – something we realised was super-important once we added a second child into the mix where time was, and is, extremely limited. He has certain hobbies, interests and self-care practices, such as tennis club, yoga and early morning walks, and so do I, with gym classes twice a week, a fortnightly massage and evening jogs. We actively encourage each other to prioritise these without any 'you owe me' comeback.

The result is that we are extremely grateful to the other for taking over the reins of the household, so that we each have the time to thrive and grow, and we are visibly reinvigorated. Equally, we carve out time for just us. Even if it's once a week on a Friday night, we make sure we give each other that time unconditionally to be together and to regroup at the end of a busy week – even if that means saying no to a lads/ladies soirée at times. It does take some thought, patience and planning, but trust me, working on your interdependent relationship is a game-changer.

Depending on the status of your relationship, a few other things to reflect on when it comes to the topic of interdependence are your thoughts on sharing certain things, such as bank accounts, cars, clothes, personal space, friends and even family. It might sound a bit weird, but there are certain things that some people just do not like to share.

I have a friend who is happily married, and has been for several years, but her husband and her have separate bank accounts, with no joint account for anything. They are both quite private (and independent) when it comes to finances, and even though they openly share their money and financial information with each other, they choose to keep what they have separate. Fortunately, they both agree on this, but it could cause conflict in another couple who have different ideas about what elements of interdependence they feel are important.

Have these conversations, even if they feel a bit silly, to establish where each other sits with the various aspects of the 'sharing' part an interdependent relationship brings. It's often the most trivial things that can throw up the biggest surprises or irks. (I once had a boyfriend who liked to share toothbrushes, which wasn't for me!) Embrace who you are and celebrate who you are as a couple. That's the magic recipe, so let's work on that shared goal.

Creating interdependent couple goals

This exercise will serve as your #CoupleGoals. A relationship always needs to know where it's heading and you need to work as a team to create that vision and shared goals. The goals can be updated too once they have been reached – it helps to keep things fresh and you both actively working on your relationship as a life priority.

- Each take a piece of paper and first write down 'What matters to me.' List all the things which are important to you and what you'd like your partner to respect and be mindful of.
- Next write down 'I need, I want' – two very different asks but both important. Be honest and jot down what you 'need' and 'want' from both your own individual perspective and your couple perspective. We forget sometimes exactly what we want and need to feel fulfilled, so writing it down and sharing it with your partner brings that crystal-clear clarity for all. It's also helpful to add a 'why' in there, too. Examples might be: 'I need time and space to unwind from work each week, and I need one-to-one time as a couple to do something fun and meaningful' or 'I want a night out with just my mates to cut loose, and I want a romantic day together to reconnect'.
- Once you're both super-clear on what each other needs and wants, create your interdependent couple goal. Brainstorm on a piece of paper where you're both heading. Factor in personal growth goals for each of you outside the relationship and create joint goals where you're both on the same team, heading in the same direction, reaching for the same thing.

An example of one client couple's interdependent goal plans is for her: 'Playing netball once a week, seeing girlfriends regularly, going to the gym two or three times a week.' For him: 'Golf with the lads every Saturday, yoga twice a week.' And their joint goal is: 'Sunday couple day = take it in turns to cook for each other, country walk, movie, work on house renovation ideas together.'

This couple used to spend so much time in each other's company that they were getting grouchy and resentful with being too much in each other's pockets. Re-establishing what each of them needed to feel fulfilled in and out of the relationship has overhauled them dramatically. They now enjoy missing each other when the other is out having independent time and they really look forward to the meaningful moments they carve out together as a couple.

What 'tis to love

You've gotta love Shakespeare, who once said, 'Love looks not with the eyes, but with the mind, and therefore is wing'd Cupid painted blind.' This is such a great quote and so true! Love is so much more than a feeling: it's an action, a verb, it's something that we *do* to ensure the people around us feel cherished. We can all look at our other half and trot out the words 'I love you' and for the most part I don't doubt it's meant with feeling, but it's also important to show our love in other ways and to communicate with our partner in the right 'love language'.

Dr Gary Chapman is an American author, speaker and marriage counsellor. He is most known for his bestselling book, *The 5 Love Languages*, a terrific book which has honestly been a game-changer in my own marriage. Love languages are all about working out communication preferences within a relationship. Dr Chapman suggests that there are five ways in which we show and receive our love.

These are:

Giving praise (words of affirmation): This means verbal acknowledgements of affection, such as 'I love you', as well as words of appreciation and encouragement. This can also include digital communication like texting or emailing. These expressions make the recipient feel understood and appreciated.

Spending time together (quality time): Spending time together, giving your partner your undivided attention with no distractions, and being fully in the present moment makes the recipient feel special and number one.

Doing nice things for your partner (acts of service): Doing something for your partner shows you care. This is the 'actions speak louder than words' way of communicating and it doesn't have to be big things. Bringing a cup of tea in the morning, loading the dishwasher without being asked, bringing a hot water bottle when you're feeling poorly – just because it would make your life easier. Some people feel more comfortable showing their love by doing.

Giving presents (gifts): This doesn't just mean getting a whacking great present to show one's affection, it's about the thought that counts. A pebble from a special beach, flowers on a particular day, a note tucked into your workbag... People who value gifts as a love language value these visual symbols of love.

Physical affection (physical touch): Many people feel emotionally connected and loved when they receive physical signs of affection such as kissing, cuddling, handholding and, of course, sex. This doesn't have to be a blatant PDA, but simply kissing your partner on the cheek as you walk past or a touching shoulder squeeze can make all the difference to someone who values physical affection.

The key with using love languages in your relationship is to first identify what *your* love language is and how you like to receive love, and then to identify what *your partner's* love language is so you can serve each other best. This isn't about playing mind tricks on each other or trying to second-guess your partner; it's about wanting to learn from each other, being curious about what makes each other tick, and being open to exploring each other's love language preference, especially if you both have different ones.

Ask yourselves, How you feel loved? What means the most to you? Imagine some everyday scenarios with your partner and what could happen to make you feel considered and appreciated? Do you melt when you have a long, cosy cuddle? Are you tickled pink when you get a thoughtful present for no reason? Is your day made if your partner does the chores without asking? This is how you decipher which is your primary and secondary love language. My number one is acts of service: honestly, if him indoors so much as runs me a bath I'm putty in his hands. And my number two is words of affirmation: a little text in the day to say he's thinking of me makes me skip like a little girl in delight.

Have a play with love languages. It's not a relationship miracle-worker, but it's a great way to improve how we express ourselves and communicate, and for many the payoff is quite extraordinary and almost instant. Learning to love your partner in the right way and, more importantly, learning how best to show it, can take your relationship to the next level.

The C word (shhh it's 'compromise')

There comes a time in all relationships when a healthy dose of compromise is going to be needed. It can irk and it can ruffle feathers at times, but all couples need to work with eachother – and share who is doing the compromising.

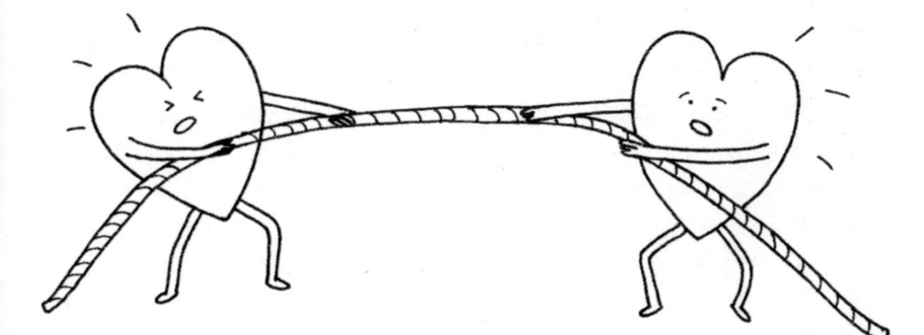

Someone who feels they have had to compromise a lot can often feel a bit hard done by, as though they always have to be the one to back down, and a better understanding of how it can be done so nobody feels aggrieved can do wonders for a relationship.

Give and take is a huge part of couples coaching. It requires good communication, authenticity (i.e. being 'real' and transparent) from both sides and a big dollop of hard work. It also helps if any ego or defensive behaviour is left firmly at the door. It's not about winning or feeling like you've lost, although there are certainly some scenarios which might make you feel like that (the choice of the new family car, for instance), but it's always worth remembering that feeling so you know how to react fairly when the tables are turned next time.

There are lots of situations which mean that couples need to meet in the middle. Sometimes it's easier said than done. There are some things we can defer to our partner on (like the aforementioned car perhaps), and there are others we can't and, importantly, shouldn't.

Compromise taps massively into our values system: what is important to us and what beliefs we hold. It might be easier to come to an agreement on what to watch on the telly for instance, than it might be to tolerate a partner's certain hobby.

I have a friend who feels very much like a 'footy widow' due to her husband's absence at the weekends chasing the big game, and another got so fed up with her driveway resembling an episode of *Wheeler Dealers* due to her partner's car restoration hobby she ended up renting him a garage in the next town!

It might be fairly easy to work out how you spend your weekends together and to alternate family Christmases, but it might be impossible to compromise on whether or not you want children, or your religious faith or political views.

How to deal with conflicting values

When I work with couples who have conflicting values, the key is not to butt heads in order to get one to change (big lesson here: we can't and shouldn't change someone), but to try to persuade them to 'agree to disagree'; to respect the other's viewpoint, and understand how and why that value might be held in high regard. Then compromise and communication can help bridge the gap where any values are misaligned.

An example of this is a couple who have conflicting attitudes around the value of forgiveness. In the past, one half of the couple has been badly hurt emotionally by someone else and they find forgiveness hard. The other half of the couple holds forgiveness as an important value due to their own past life experiences and faith, and struggles to understand or accept their partner's perceived inability to forgive.

In all other areas the couple have shared values, but this one is like a thorn in their sides and causes conflict. The solution: to communicate, understand and respect each other's viewpoint, and accept that each other's feelings are valid and unique, and that there are some situations where forgiveness is difficult. In this situation I'd encourage the couple to keep working on what forgiveness means to them both and how they can both be a little more flexible with their expectations of each other around this value.

Outlining what's important to you and anything that is an absolute 'no budge' situation to your partner is necessary in order to work out the parameters. It is then up to your partner to decide how they feel and what's important to them in turn. This two-way communication is so vital as it can help dissipate any tension. How many of us act as if we are compromising on something, but actually what we're doing is caving in to avoid a scene or an argument, or just because it's easier in the moment? There will be moments when this feels like the most appropriate course of action, but it absolutely needs to be addressed as soon as possible before it gets swept under the carpet and resentment and habit bed in.

I remember being caught out during a 'who's drinking/driving?' tête-à-tête at a friends' wedding (so many of us can relate), where I 'compromised' by agreeing to be the designated driver 'this time' as it was his mate's wedding. Did I compromise though? Not really. I just backed down because we were having one of those 'talking and smiling through gritted teeth' arguments in front of friends and were teetering dangerously close to being fun sponges, so I just took one for the team before it got embarrassing. A nice thing to do you might say, and yes it was, but secretly I felt a bit pissed off and put out. As though I'd 'lost'.

And that's exactly what we don't want from compromise. With the benefit of hindsight, we could have avoided any awkwardness and me feeling naffed off purely by having the chat and working out the parameters before the event. Planning! A fair, sensible conversation (which we now make sure we have) would have allowed us to agree on some give and take when it comes to going-out responsibilites.

Compromise is so much more than just working out a way to resolve something together; it's about really understanding where the other is coming from and doing all you can to reach a decision that is fair to both. Depending on personalities, particularly if one of you falls into a classic 'people pleaser' personality trait, one of you may find compromise a lot easier than the other.

This doesn't have to be a massive problem, particularly with the small stuff, but if it becomes a little bit of a pattern, where one of you simply gives in in order to keep the peace without a proper conversation and mutual understanding, resentment and an unhealthy balance could start brewing.

Try focusing on how something makes you feel, instead of just the situation. Put your thoughts across from your 'first person' perspective: 'I feel...' or 'What this means to me is...' etc. Be honest about what you're finding hard and any reasons attached to it. It will help your partner understand your point of view and there's a greater chance of them being empathetic. Let your partner know they are able to talk in the same way and that you will equally listen to them.

When you're both talking openly and honestly and in a measured way about the situation, you're more likely to find a way forwards and make a decision that is fair to you both. Often it's not about the particular situation; it's about not feeling heard or listened to, or having our feelings respected when it comes to being able to, or even wanting to, compromise.

I receive hundreds of messages from people fed up with their relationship due to compromise clashes, and top of the list of complaints when it comes to giving and taking are 'time' (equal quality time together and separate) and 'feelings' (wanting to be listened to and respected more).

Work together as a team to compromise on the small stuff, and outline the big stuff, such as religion, attitudes around drink and drugs, and having a family etc., early doors. When you feel heard and understood, it is far easier to reach a compromise where nobody feels they have had the raw end of the deal. It's also a cherry on the cake to be verbally and physically grateful to the other person for meeting you halfway.

Relationships are a constant relay race. You take the baton, run with it for a bit, then pass it over to your teammate when it's necessary for them to do their bit. It's not about who crosses the finish line, it's about everything that's gone into the race as a team. And we all drop the baton from time to time. That's just being real and human, but what winners (as it were) do is pick it up, dust themselves off and get back on (the) track together.

> “I bl**dy hate compromising with my wife! She gloats as if she's won, which just makes me want to dig my heels in and do what I wanted to do in the first place!”
>
> Andrew, 43

Great expectations

A great way to gain perspective on a situation is to imagine it playing out as a movie scene and to take on the vantage point of an observer, a third person sitting at a distance watching the situation play out.

This trick removes you from the scenario and gives you the chance to be more objective about what you notice. It can be very useful in adjusting expectations and rigid thinking in a conflict, as you can put yourself in both yours and your partner's shoes.

Maybe you've reached a stalemate and need to gain some much-needed insight and clarity on how to move things forward.

- Sit yourself somewhere comfortable and close your eyes.
- Imagine the relationship situation that needs some assistance. First imagine it from your own perspective, as if you were sitting or standing facing your partner and playing over what the issue is. For example, an argument about where you'd like to go on holiday.
- Next, switch roles and play out that scene from your partner's position. Explore what they're feeling and present their side of the situation as they look back at 'you'.
- Next, in your mind's eye, take a step or float to a corner in the room, away from you both, so you can see the pair of you in the situation.
- Simply sit or stand and watch the pair of you from that vantage point and ask yourself what you notice. What do you see? How do you feel about the pair of them? Him? Her? What are each of them saying, thinking and feeling?
- As the observer, regard the issue as someone who wants the best for you both. Someone who is impartial. And weigh up and explore the differing viewpoints to find empathy and compromise.
- Encourage your partner to do the same and see how they find it? This exercise can help calm a heated situation, especially where heads are butting. Exploring the three different vantage points helps both of you to fully listen and be listened to back – which is most of the battle won!

Core values list

Acceptance
Accomplishment
Achievement
Acquisition
Adventure
Alignment
Altruism
Ambitious
Amusement
Assistance
Attractiveness
Authenticity
Awareness

Beauty
Being
Bliss

Calm
Capable
Charity
Cheerful
Coach
Community
Compassion
Comprehending
Connection
Consciousness
Connection
Consciousness
Consideration
Constancy
Contentment
Contribution
Cooperation
Courage
Creativity

Dependability
Dignity
Direct
Discovery
Diversity

Economic security
Education
Effectiveness
Elegance
Emotional wellbeing
Empathy
Encourage
Encouragement
Energy
Enlightenment
Entertainment
Environment
Equality
Ethics/ethical
Excellence
Experiment
Expertise
Explain
Exquisiteness

Facilitation
Fairness
Faith
Fame
Family
Feeling good
Fitness
Forgiving
Freedom
Friendship
Fun

Generosity
Grace
Gratitude
Guidance

Happiness
Hard-working
Harmony
Health
Helpful
Honesty
Honour
Hope
Humility

Imagination
Improvement
Independence
Influence
Information
Inner peace
Innovation
Inspiration
Instruction
Integrity
Intelligence
Inventiveness

Joy
Justice

Kindness
Knowledge

Laughter
Leadership
Learning
Love
Loyalty

Magnificence
Mastery
Merriment

Nobility
Nutrition

Obedient
Open-minded
Order
Organisation
Originality

Peace
Peacefulness
Perception
Personal development

Play
Pleasure
Positive attitude
Power
Preparation
Presence
Proficiency
Provider

Quest

Radiance
Rational
Recognition
Relatedness
Relationships
Relaxation
Reliability
Religious/religion
Resourcefulness
Respect
Responsibility
Responsiveness
Risk

Safety
Schooling
Self-awareness
Self-control
Self-worth
Sensations
Sensuality
Serenity
Service
Simplicity
Spirituality
Stability
Stimulation
Strength
Strengthen
Success
Superiority
Support

Teaching
Tenderness
Touch
Tranquility
Trust
Truth/truthfulness

Understanding

Victory
Vision

Wealth
Wholeness
Winning
Wisdom

8

WHEN ALL IS SAID AND DONE

'The opposite of love isn't hate, it's indifference.'
Elie Wiesel, human rights activist

This book is about nurturing and loving yourself, as well as your love life. It needs to be a collaboration between working on yourself and within your couple in order to create a happy and healthy relationship. But it is also about being real, being honest, and having the awareness to recognise when things need work and changing.

Good relationships can be utterly wonderful. They enrich our lives and we all gain so much from having people we love and who in turn love us. But some relationships don't last and recognising when a relationship is not serving any positive purpose any more is important. Sometimes we can't make ourselves fit together and we just gotta cut loose for the sake of our future.

Many of us are guilty of letting a romance linger for fear of confrontation, or the situation being awkward or painful, or the habit of being with a particular someone just becomes the 'easier' option. I know many people who stay in lacklustre relationships because they simply 'can't be arsed' to change them. The fact is, breakups can be painful for everybody involved, there is no easy way around them and avoidance often just makes the whole situation worse.

If you find moving on from a relationship tricky, or struggle to know when you should or shouldn't throw the towel in, trust me you're not alone. First, it's important to identify *if* there is anything that can be done to salvage the partnership. There has to be will, effort and motivation from both sides. Second, if things have gone too far down a dead end, then there are ways to go about ending a relationship which can feel a little less crap – for both of you.

Let's look at some of the challenges that can threaten a relationship, how to handle a rocky patch and when it's perhaps time to face facts that it's the end of the road.

Break up or make up?

The first thing that's important to know is that having relationship issues doesn't necessarily mean it's your fault or that you're not very good at relationships. There are so many reasons why couples hit testing times, as we've explored in this book, and I honestly can't stress enough how important it is to go easy on yourself.

Even the best relationships have ups and downs, so never feel like you're failing if you hit some rough times along the way. Some things you can work out and some things you just can't – even with all the will in the world. This chapter is about being OK with that and not allowing any negativity to spoil your future – whether you decide to stay with your current partner, move on to another partner or become a nun. There's no judgement here.

To make up or break up, that is the question? Ultimately only you will know and can decide on whether a relationship is something worth fighting for or if it's the end of the road. What's acceptable in one person's relationship won't be in the next, so never measure yours against anyone else's – they have their own sets of values, beliefs and boundaries to work with. What *you* might not like, might not be a problem for the next couple.

I had a client who had a major issue with their partner using expletives (f and c bombs) when things got heated. He thought there was nothing wrong with it and regarded it as just an expression of his frustration. She, however, found it disrespectful. They came to me wanting some help managing conflict and both wanted me to 'side' with them on the language issue (him: it's not a big deal, her: it's a big deal).

Now obviously, as a coach, I stayed impartial, but the lesson to get across to them was that it didn't matter if *I* thought she or he were being unreasonable, it was how *they* felt in their relationship as a result of it and what might happen if things didn't change.

Some work on learned behaviour (he'd grown up in a family where colourful language was the norm; her mother was a primary school teacher and bad language was not used or tolerated), boundaries (what each of them felt was and wasn't OK) and communication (explaining the situation from each one's perspective and actively listening to each other) saw these guys in a much happier place with some more helpful tools to work their way through conflict. Left undealt with, this issue would have led to a premature end to their marriage.

This is why tapping into your individual and couple values and beliefs is so helpful. It will act as an antenna when things get a bit sticky and when you're curled up clutching your glass of vino in a post-bicker rage, fantasising about a singleton life, or if you're married perhaps dreaming of divorce; it will help you objectively work through (when you've calmed down) what you can, need and want to do for your happiness.

When the end is nigh

There can be many reasons for ending a relationship, but whatever these come down to it will undoubtedly be upsetting. Many couples decide as a last-ditch attempt to save the relationship to have couples therapy and it's often very successful, although both parties have to want it to work and fully commit to the process, and it's important to be honest about your feelings and intentions towards each other.

Sometimes, though, you've just checked out and there's no way back. And as sad as that can be, we can't fake our feelings – if you've got the ick, you've got the ick.

There are, of course, various routes by which a relationship might come to the point where the best course of action is to call it a day, including serious issues such as controlling behaviour, narcissism (an inflated sense of one's own importance and a lack of empathy for others) and any type of abuse (physical, verbal, domestic, sexual, financial), as well as drug abuse or excessive drunkenness.

Another big reason for a relationship to end is adultery, and cheating on a partner is widely recognised in society as a major no when it comes to a committed relationship. Some couples do manage to work through infidelity. In fact, I know plenty who have (it takes honesty, forgiveness and work), but equally many people can't, as forgiving and forgetting just isn't possible for them.

The decision on whether a couple can work through any of these issues is ultimately down to the individuals involved; it's deeply personal. Taking counsel and advice from friends and family *can* sometimes be useful, but do so with caution. Having your mates slag off your partner isn't the most helpful thing to hear when you're emotionally wrung out and trying to work out your next move forward.

So how do you know when to fight for it or call it a day? That, my friend, is your decision. You know by now what you can, will and won't tolerate. Remind yourself of what's important to you, what your goals are and where you're heading, and use this self-empowered clarity to weigh up the importance of your partner and relationship. What would life look like with or without them in it?

To know whether you want to work things out, ask yourself: 'What were we doing differently when it was going well?' and 'Is there a way to do more of this as a way to improve things?' Relationships have lots of good bits and some not so good bits. It's worth considering whether there's enough 'good' to outweigh the 'not so good'.

It's a fact that when there are kids in the picture and their wellbeing as well as issues like living arrangements and financial obligations are involved, a lot of couples make the decision that the practicalities and damage limitation of staying together outweigh anything else. One should never 'just settle' and be miserable in a relationship which is dead. However, these are very real concerns for a lot of couples when deciding what they're going to do.

No person or relationship will ever be perfect. It's about being good enough. Focus on that and the answer on which way you'll turn should hopefully become clearer.

> “We grew apart and even though I still loved him the spark had just died. We had buried our dissatisfaction for so long that when we finally did something about it, it was too late. I'm sad we're over, but we just couldn't get it back.”
>
> Annalise, 38

Remember, remember...

When relationships hit the skids and perhaps frustration, bitterness and resentment seep in, it can be difficult to feel positive, or even willing, to try to fix things.

Rekindling that initial love and connection can be tough, especially if things have been on a downward turn for some time, but it's absolutely possible to get back to a more agreeable and upbeat place. Your most valuable tool is your mind and, more specifically, your memory.

This technique can be hugely beneficial for couples who have lost their way and are hoping to get back on track. It can evoke all the 'feels' that might have been a bit 'MIA' in recent times and it can help re-establish why a couple fell in love in the first place, cancelling out any of the unhelpful 'noise' that may have been masking it.

- Time to take a trip down memory lane. Have all your five senses at the ready and sit down with your partner.

- Take a few minutes to each think back to the time you first met. Close your eyes as you let the memory come back to the forefront of your mind.
- As the memory plays out, absorb yourself in everything you can see, feel, hear, taste and smell. Re-create the memory and put yourself back in the moment.
- What can you see? What are your first impressions of each other? What do you notice about them? How do they make you feel? What else do you notice about the scenario? Can you hear any particular music or sounds? Is there a familiar or defining smell that you remember – the surroundings, food, perfume?
- Enjoy the moment and the memory, and then share what you remember with each other, enjoying the finer details and incidentals that may crop up from each perspective.
- Allow yourselves to notice what you were feeling then and how you can utilise some of those thoughts and behaviours again now in the present. Based on that shared defining moment, make a plan for how you can embrace what attracted and brought you both together then, and bring that plan into the here and now, and on to a shared future.

If the 'first meeting' isn't a strong enough memory, you may like to choose another defining moment such as your wedding day, honeymoon, a holiday, birth of a child or the first time you said, 'I love you' – whatever helps get you both back to the root of your romance to bring the learning forward.

Using our subconscious mind and our memories to ignite the feel-good hormones is a great technique we can all use. Going on a sensory memory journey together can really help when a relationship is losing sight of what is sacred and special, and it's an effective way to leave the crap at the door for a bit, while you get back to basics, and work out what you have together and if it's worth saving.

Beating cheating

Being unfaithful isn't always about sex. We tend to pigeonhole cheating as just having sex with another person outside of a relationship. Of course, this is a big part of infidelity, but there are many other reasons why our relationship might get into difficulty and where one, or even both, feel the need to 'go elsewhere'.

Cheating on your partner isn't just about physically being unfaithful. Lots of people can be emotionally unfaithful too. In fact, studies suggest that the main reasons for seeking solace in another person don't actually involve sex at all. It might end up becoming a part of it, but often the trigger for looking elsewhere is emotionally, not physically, led. People cheat because they feel angry, have self-esteem issues, feel unloved, feel neglected or are in a difficult or specific situation, for example stressed or drunk.

It's fair to say that infidelity is complicated and for those involved it comes with a whole load of emotional baggage. Sure, the initial exhilaration of having your needs met can be all-consuming. It's true that the thrill often outweighs other feelings in the initial throes of temptation and tasting the forbidden fruit, but when the excitement gives way to a big slap in the face of reality, the real complications surface.

If you've ever been cheated on you will no doubt identify with the gut-wrenching, vomit-inducing pain it brings with it. Perhaps you have been the 'cheater' and if so I'm sure there were reasons, perhaps even justifications, for your actions. You'll find no judgement here, only an opportunity to reflect and learn. If two people are feeling happy, loved, respected and fulfilled in a relationship, there shouldn't be any chinks in the chain that could lead to seeing if the grass is greener on the other side.

Lots of people I've spoken to over the years who have been open enough to admit when their wandering eye has become a potential problem report feeling bored in their relationship. Some have felt neglected by their partner, sidelined due to work/kids/life and not made to feel attractive any more, so have gratefully received any compliments (and advances) from outside the relationship.

Others feel the release of escapism that having an affair can bring. Perhaps life has become stressful or overwhelming, and the prospect of seeking solace emotionally and/or physically in another person acts as a release. Let's also be honest, there are also some people who are just cheating buggers, who want to try their luck at having their cake and eating it with no regard whatsoever for their partner, and who feel no remorse or guilt for their actions.

It can be very easy to judge somebody who has committed an act of adultery and there is no getting away from the fact that within the realms of an official commitment it is wrong, unfair and unkind. But things are often far more complicated than they appear and in my experience of helping people who have been affected by cheating in a relationship, there is often more to it than simply wanting to be an unfaithful rogue.

Some people, typically those lacking love in their main relationship, aren't even concerned about being caught. It can be part of their desperate attempts to communicate with their partner about what they need and are lacking, and sometimes they use getting caught as their exit strategy.

According to a report by *Psychology Today*, in the majority of cases the affair just fizzles out and, perhaps surprisingly, only one in five relationships end because of an affair. Some reports suggest that 70% of couples actually stay together, even when they have found out that their partner has cheated. The remaining relationships tend to break up for non-cheating reasons.

Whatever the situation, there is no doubting that being unfaithful in a relationship is never a good idea. Someone usually gets hurt and it can create a whole load of unwanted pain and stress. I'm certainly not here to wag my finger, because we are all human, we all have needs and urges, and we all make mistakes – but we all know that cheating isn't as straightforward as simply seeking sex.

Just knowing this can be helpful in recognising the importance of working on the emotional connection in our partnerships. This will undoubtedly help you feel more satisfied, close to and stable with your partner, and it will hopefully help ensure you both stay faithful to each other and aren't prompted to 'seek solace' elsewhere.

"After having our twins I just didn't have any time for myself anymore, let alone my partner. I barely looked at him. I found some flirty messages on his phone and it was like a dagger to my heart. He admitted he'd been feeling neglected and had been talking to someone at his work. We both wanted to make things work, so we got some help. We talked properly for the first time in ages and we're definitely getting back some of the spark and trust. It's a slow process, but we want it to work."

Stacey, 33

Don't you want me baby

Working on our emotional connection gives a flailing relationship a darn good go at getting back on track. A lot of people report feeling a bit bored in the bedroom and we've all heard of that clichéd 'seven year itch'. Sex isn't the be all and end all of a relationship – companionship can be much more important in a lot of cases – but many couples do need a bit of a helping hand to pep things up between the sheets.

Don't ever automatically see this as a failure or as though there's something wrong. Anything we do over and over again can lose its shine a bit. I adore going on rollercoasters, but after the umpteenth loop I've rather lost some of the initial enthusiasm!

Get that interest and enthusiasm back by making a few tweaks here and there, which can help ignite the passion again. As long as there is a base level of attraction, the rest can be worked on. Rediscover the finer fun sides of each other and put some effort into your (making) love life. You might find that one thing leads to another (nudge nudge, wink wink).

- Each write down date ideas on separate bits of paper. They don't have to be fancy (some can be), but essentially opportunities to spend time together.
- Think outside the box. Dinner and drinks, Netflix and chill – it's all very nice, but also very predictable. What else could you do together to ensure it's quality time? It doesn't have to cost a fortune either. In fact some the best dates are the cheapest.
- Some ideas are: massage night in, cook a meal together, wine or beer tasting, go bowling, ice skating or a bike ride, go for a scenic walk with a hot chocolate, a picnic in the park, enjoy an evening class together...
- Write down all your date ideas and put them in a box or jar. Agree a time you can dedicate to each other consistently, for instance every other Saturday night, and discuss anything which might need to be considered in order for you both to be able to stick to the plans, e.g. booking a babysitter, booking time off a work rota etc.
- Allowing enough time for any planning, each of you 'lucky dip' to pick a date suggestion and look forward to planning and spending that focused time together.

Quality time together massively helps in rekindling that romantic spark. You may want to go one step further and try popping some bedroom 'sexy time' ideas into the jar, too, to help boost your sex life. Communicate on what you'd like from the relationship, explore each other intimately and perhaps try new things which you're both up for giving a go.

This demonstrates it's a team effort; you're both keeping it fresh and evolving, and that's a huge part of keeping connected and the relationship together.

The love triangle

Most of us have heard of love triangles. I've even been in one myself, albeit at the age of nine in primary school when my unrequited love for a boy called Christopher was Nicola in Year 8's gain when she became his girlfriend instead. Princess Diana also once famously spoke of her own love triangle tussle. Here the 'love triangle' I'm talking about is a little bit different. It's American psychologist Robert Sternberg's Triangular Theory of Love, something which, when it comes to relationships, can be very insightful.

Sternberg's interesting and yet basic theory is that there are three components that matter in *every* relationship (not just romantic ones) and it's how much of those three ingredients you have that define the type of relationship. This is similar to the 'ingredients' we talked about in chapter 5 and how romantic relationships require friendship, connection and attraction. Robert Sternberg goes one step further and suggests the components needed for *any* type of relationship, which is really interesting to ponder when you're considering your own relationship status.

According to the psychologist a relationship needs a combination of the following:

- Intimacy
- Passion
- Commitment

And depending on how much of each of the three ingredients are present, there are seven different relationship outcomes. In short, these are:

Liking: When you experience a lot of intimacy with someone, but you don't feel any passion for them or a desire to spend the rest of your life with them.

Infatuated love: When you feel only passion towards that person, but not much intimacy or commitment. It can come and go quickly.

Empty love: When there is a lot of commitment (perhaps a long-term marriage) holding the relationship together, but the levels of intimacy and passion have dwindled.

Romantic love: When you bond emotionally and physically with someone, but there's a low level of commitment, meaning there isn't any longevity in the couple. A passionate fling perhaps.

Companionate love: When a couple share intimacy and commitment, but the passion and physical attraction side of the relationship has waned.

Fatuous love: When the relationship has perhaps been a whirlwind romance and the couple have fallen madly in love and married soon after. However, the intimacy, which is needed to build lasting foundations, is missing.

Consummate love: When all three ingredients are highly present in a romantic relationship in equal measures. This is referred to as 'complete love'. It's the sweet spot, the holy grail and it must be guarded carefully.

Which of these describes your relationship? And which describes the relationship you'd like to have? This is a book about relationships and I find from my own personal and professional experience that this can be a really useful measure of all the relationships you welcome into your life, not just the romantic ones. The Triangular Theory of Love can serve as a helpful guide when things are going awry in your love life, and give you an indicator of what needs to change or be worked on.

Therapy isn't a dirty word

Therapy is often unfairly stigmatised, but thankfully with mental health being talked about more freely and post-pandemic vulnerability affecting everyone, seeking help from a trained professional has become a lot more accepted. Relationship or couples therapy (sometimes also referred to as coaching or counselling) is slowly becoming more commonplace and less shrouded in embarrassment, stigma and failure.

Our American cousins have been far more open and accepting of relationship intervention and there's much less taboo surrounding it, but the UK is thankfully catching up. And with good reason, because the statistics speak for themselves. According to the American Association for Marriage and Family Therapy, a whopping 93% of their clients said they were able to deal with marital problems more effectively after receiving counselling.

The UK's largest provider of relationship support, Relate, also reports that in 2020 it helped over 2 million people of all ages, backgrounds, sexual orientations and gender identities to strengthen their relationships. It's fantastic to know so many people are now reaching out asking for help and support when they need it. There's no shame in it.

When might you think about seeking couples therapy? And where do you go and what happens? Couples coaching is actually beneficial from as early as when you realise there's a future in store for you both. Pre-marital counselling is a real thing and a really important part of preparing for your future together as a couple. So many people focus on the wedding, with very little thought given to what happens *after* the big day, and working on the whole point of why you are choosing to be together and what that will look and be like is key for a positive start.

Pre-marital counselling helps you both learn skills and strategies that you can use to prevent possible problems in the future. With a trained therapist you'll celebrate your relationship and identify its strengths, and then using those strengths work on making the relationship even better and stronger. You can also expect to talk about any challenges you might face and how to overcome them productively. Pre-marital counsellors or coaches can be accessed in a few ways. Churches or religious groups often offer pre-marriage courses. There are online therapists and most counsellors registered with professional organisations such as the British Association for Counselling and Psychotherapy (BACP) will offer relationship therapy for any stage of your relationship.

Other times you might feel the benefit of contacting a therapist for couples help are when:

- You're constantly fighting/arguing
- You're avoiding conflict
- You're disagreeing over money matters
- There's a lack of intimacy (emotional and/or physical)
- Someone has cheated
- You're considering divorce

What you're likely to get from couples therapy is down to the commitment of you both, how seriously you take it and your joint motivation to succeed. You're likely to learn about:

- Improving your communication, including actively listening and talking
- Defining expectations from each other and establishing boundaries

- Interdependency – how to spend meaningful time together and apart
- Re/building trust, especially if there has been breach of trust in the relationship

Couples therapy, like any form of talking therapy, can cost anything from free (if it's from a certain charity or on the NHS), right up to hundreds of pounds, depending on the therapist's level of qualification. As a good rough guide, reckon on spending anything between £50 and £100 for a session, which is usually an hour (sometimes one and a half hours for the initial session).

Sessions can be face to face in person, via video call or a voice call, or by email. It's up to you to decide what type you'd prefer and to factor variables such as time, distance and cost in to your decision-making. I have a client couple up in the remotest northern point of the UK who I coach via video call. It's a fantastic way of accessing services that would otherwise be out of reach.

Always ask your therapist first how much they charge for a session and how many they might recommend so you can work out your budget. It's not uncommon to have several sessions before you really start to do some change work. However, you're in charge and are welcome to commit to one or a hundred sessions if you so wish. Private counsellors or therapists are usually fairly available to book, but if you are accessing free or subsidised counselling you may find yourself on a waiting list.

If even after you've gone through couples counselling in an attempt to repair relationship breakdown it just can't be worked through, try not to feel that the sessions have been wasted. Any chance you take to try and make something work should always be met with praise and respect, even if the outcome is the end of the road.

There are times when the aim of couples counselling isn't for the duo to stay together. A lot of couples want to, and try to, split amicably and a therapist can really help with this process of (to use a Gwyneth Paltrow classic) 'uncoupling'. Relationships are likely have been built over time and the couple's lives will inevitably be intertwined, so it stands to reason that finances, homes, possessions, children, pets etc. will be part of the equation.

Couples who end up saying their farewells after going through couples therapy generally feel more appeased, calmer and in a better place emotionally than if they hadn't gone through the process. Ending a relationship is a hot mess of emotions – anger, upset, regret, guilt, sorrow, sadness, confusion – and having that dedicated time and space to vent and let any negative emotions out can be hugely cathartic. It can also enable both sides to leave the relationship having drawn a line under it and move forward burden-free.

Breaking up is rarely easy, so the main thing to remember is that it's your situation, your feelings, and don't measure your experiences against anyone else's. Most importantly, be kind to yourself as you process it and heal.

My achy breaky heart

Ending a relationship is one of the most difficult things we might have to do in life, but let's face facts: there are times when staying together just isn't the best outcome and the end of the road has come. Nearly 50% of marriages end in divorce, and there are, of course, more casual and common-law partnerships that also decide to call it a day.

Being involved in a breakup is crap. I've certainly been on the receiving end of a few and it can hurt like hell. The old adage, time is a healer, certainly does ring true in most cases and I can honestly say that every single breakup I have been through definitely feels less painful now than it did then. In fact, I don't give those painful times a second thought, that's how brilliant a healer time can be.

Knowing how to break up well can really help make the whole process much easier, smoother and less harmful for both partners. Let's be clear: there is no 'right' or 'wrong' way to break up and there certainly isn't a 'best' way either, but recognising that every person and every relationship is unique and different, and certain needs should be considered, can really help make it a little more bearable.

We need to be realistic; breaking up can be a very upsetting experience and your emotions can take a knock. Being prepared for this can actually really help to process the situation, so acknowledge and accept that there will be emotional pain. It's like any loss we experience in life – we need to go through it in order to deal with it. Simply ignoring it and leapfrogging over it rarely helps us move forward in a healthy way.

Don't ghost: One of the worst things we can do is to finish a relationship via text or email, or even worse just ignore the person in the hope it fizzles out, known as ghosting. Being on the receiving end of being dumped in this way feels absolutely dreadful. It shows a complete lack of respect and consideration, a lack of giving that person the dignity of being told in person, and is extremely hurtful and confusing. Of course, breaking up in person can feel awkward, but at the very least you will be respected (or can respect yourself) for having the balls to end the relationship face to face.

Be truthful: If you've ever been on the receiving end of a breakup, you'll probably identify with wondering why. What happened? What did you do wrong? It's a horrible place to be when you question everything about why the relationship is no longer. Most of us want to know why we're being dumped and can usually handle some kind of version of the truth rather than being left in complete purgatory. Always be repectful and perhaps slightly economical with telling all if the truly honest answer would seriously hurt their feelings. No one wants to hear, 'You are crap in bed' or 'You're really boring.' Help preserve their self-esteem and confidence by phrasing things in a kind way, such as ' I don't feel we are sexually compatible' or 'I think we want different things out of life.'

Be sympathetic: Breaking up can feel really sad and if you are the one doing the breaking up the other person will probably feel significantly worse than you do at the prospect of things ending. Acknowledge that it is sad and share how you are feeling as well, so it doesn't seem one-sided. Share what you have enjoyed about your time together and if possible what positive things you will take forwards from it. A breakup often involves physical life changes as well as emotional ones – moving out of the shared home, dividing belongings, realising precious fertile years have gone by – and these can all leave someone feeling emotional and even regretful, so be kind and acknowledge any loss being experienced.

Avoid confrontation or bad feeling: It can be tempting to make a last-ditch attempt to cling onto the relationship, perhaps by trying to guilt trip the other person into staying with it. Be clear with your intentions and don't be drawn into any slagging matches or emotional blackmail. Breaking up can make people say and do some desperate things, but to avoid it dragging on any longer than it needs to, hold firm and step away from any arguments or altercations .

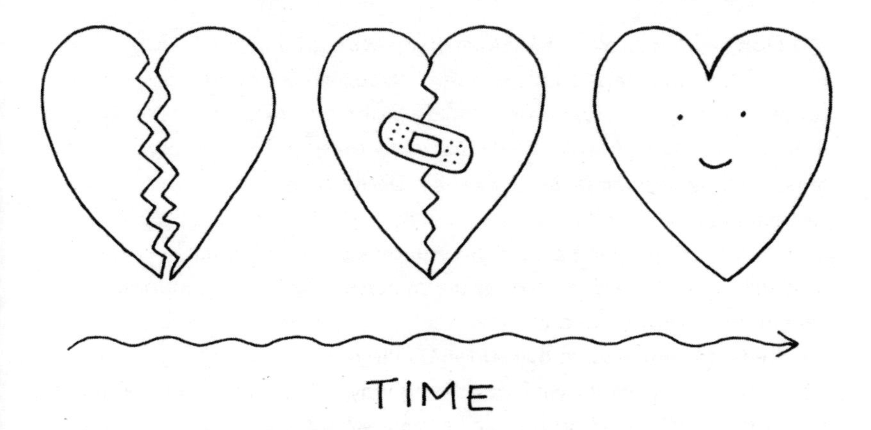

Time really is a healer: Allow yourself to grieve the end of a relationship. Even if you are the one who initiated the breakup, you may still care and think about your former partner, and you're likely to feel sad and upset. You may also feel reflective about what you had and where your life might be going next. Initially, make a clean break to help you heal, so avoid texting, calling, Facebook stalking etc. Staying friends with an ex in the early days can make it really tough to move on. It's certainly possible down the road if you both want to, but give it some space and time first.

The circle of love

And so here we are. It's been quite the journey uncovering all the elements that go into finding, and hopefully keeping, love – from dating to getting together, to finding your happy ever after, to being OK if and when things change. Perhaps you're smashing it at love, maybe you're super-happy in your relationship or yours could do with a boot up the backside. Perhaps you're navigating the dating scene like Danny Zuko in *Grease* or finding yourself in a scene with Jennifer Aniston from *The Break-Up*.

Wherever you might be in your love life remember that nothing is ever wasted. Every experience can be learned from. It's never just starting back at the beginning – every date, dalliance and relationship teaches us something. It's always really pleasing to see friends and clients realise how empowering their experiences actually are, and how they can use those experiences to keep moving forwards knowing a little more of what they want, what they don't want and, most importantly, with a greater sense of self.

The world of dating and relationships is brilliantly varied, and massively unpredictable. One of the biggest concerns people have around finding love is either not finding it or getting hurt. You've probably heard the old saying, 'It's better to have loved and lost, than never to have loved at all' and I think there's a lot of truth in that. Often it's better to feel *something* than nothing at all, and our love lives certainly serve us well there.

What it all really comes down to though is you. Whatever shape your love life takes all stems from you; you are the organ grinder not the monkey. Whatever stage you are at in life, you are in control of what you do and who with. All throughout this book we've been working on self-esteem, confidence, identity and self-worth. So really it matters not if you experience zero partners or a hundred; as long as you're happy within yourself and are comfortable regardless of having a 'significant other' or not, then that's the definition of being truly content.

Where is the love? I hope you realise by now that it's right here. You are enough. You always were and you always will be. And if you choose to let someone else in to share that love, then good for you. As Mahatma Gandhi once said, 'Where there is love, there is life,' and the beauty is it's all yours for the taking.

RESOURCES

To find out even more and to continue your relationship journey, head over to www.therelationshipplace.co.uk

Relate: The UK's largest provider of relationship support. Offers counselling, therapy and workshops.
www.relate.org.uk
0300 003 0396

Marriage Care: Marriage preparation, relationship counselling and more.
www.marriagecare.org.uk

Relationships Scotland: Scotland's largest provider of relationship counselling and family mediation.
www.relationships-scotland.org.uk
0345 119 2020

The Counselling Directory: Find a counsellor.
www.counselling-directory.org.uk

The Life Coach Directory: Find a coach or therapist.
www.lifecoach-directory.org.uk

Women's Aid: Information, support and help for domestic abuse.
www.womensaid.org.uk

Refuge: Advice and help for women and men experiencing domestic violence. Provides safe emergency accommodation.
www.refuge.org.uk

Respect Men's Advice Line: Confidential helpline and practical support for men experiencing domestic abuse.
www.mensadviceline.org.uk
0808 801 0327

Mind: The UK's leading mental health charity. Support and advice for anyone experiencing a mental health problem.
www.mind.org.uk

NHS: For any advice needed: medical, mental or anything to do with your health and wellbeing.
www.nhs.uk
111

Emergency: If you're feeling unsafe or your life is in danger.
999

References

Chapter 1

One report from website Maturity Dating suggests that there are over 15 million, https://www.maturitydating.co.uk/increased-use-online-dating/
Research from dating platform Eharmony and Imperial College Business School, https://www.eharmony.co.uk/dating-advice/dating/future-of-dating-rise-of-ebabies-digital-families/
According to the Centre of Economics and Business Research, the average date in the UK,
https://www.esquire.com/uk/life/sex-relationships/news/a13839/average-date-costs-uk/

Chapter 4

Research by Channel Mum suggests that one in five couples break up within the first year of having children, https://www.goodto.com/wellbeing/relationships/relationship-news/break-up-after-baby-513710
Rodgers, Gavin, *You're Pregnant Too, Mate! The Essential Guide for Expectant Fathers* (Robson Books, 1999)
According to the Office for National Statistics there are over half a million blended families www.ons.gov.uk/peoplepopulationandcommunity

Chapter 5

According to the Office for National Statistics, in 2018 cohabiting couples, https://www.ons.gov.uk/peoplepopulationandcommunity/birthsdeathsandmarriages/families/bulletins/familiesandhouseholds/2018
According to the Office for National Statistics divorce rates, https://www.ons.gov.uk/peoplepopulationandcommunity/birthsdeathsandmarriages/divorce/bulletins/divorcesinenglandandwales/2018
According to a report from relationship support charity Relate and YouGov, most people say that sexuality and intimate relationships, https://www.relate.org.uk/sites/default/files/the_way_we_are_now_-_lets_talk_about_sex.pdf

Chapter 6

According to YouGov, over a quarter of the UK population, https://yougov.co.uk/topics/relationships/articles-reports/2020/02/24/how-much-sex-are-britons-having

According to a report from relationship support charity Relate, https://www.relate.org.uk/sites/default/files/the_way_we_are_now_-_lets_talk_about_sex.pdf
According to research by clinical neuroscientist Dr David Weeks, https://www.telegraph.co.uk/lifestyle/10161279/Sex-is-the-secret-to-looking-younger-claims-researcher.html
...says sexual health expert and PhD Yvonne K Fullbright,
https://www.thehealthsite.com/diseases-conditions/less-sex-poor-sleep-and-other-factors-that-can-suppress-your-immune-system-788729/
...30% of women have weak pelvic floor muscles, https://www.iow.nhs.uk/Downloads/Pelvic%20Floor%20Physiotherapy/Pelvic%20Floor%20Exercise%20for%20women.pdf
Research suggests that men who ejaculate regularly,
https://sperlingprostatecenter.com/can-masturbation-help-prevent-prostate-cancer/
The most recent poll from Relate's [italics]*Let's Talk About Sex*[end italics] report,
https://www.relate.org.uk/sites/default/files/the_way_we_are_now_-_lets_talk_about_sex_0.pdf
According to the NHS, around one in seven couples, https://www.nhs.uk/conditions/infertility/

Chapter 7

Chapman, Dr Gary, (2014). *The 5 Love Languages: The Secret to Love that Lasts.* Chicago, Northfield Publishing

Chapter 8

According to a report by *Psychology Today*, in the majority of cases,
https://www.psychologytoday.com/gb/blog/fixing-families/202002/6-reasons-why-affairs-eventually-fall-apart
https://divorce.lovetoknow.com/Rates_of_Divorce_for_Adultery_and_Infidelity
Some reports suggest that 70% of couples actually stay together,
https://www.globalinvestigations.co.uk/news/infidelity-statistics-uk-infographic/
https://www.rewire.org/cheated-hope-relationship/
According to the American Association for Marriage and Family Therapy,
https://www.talkspace.com/blog/everything-you-need-to-know-about-couples-therapy/
Nearly 50% of marriages end in divorce, and there are, of course, https://www.relate.org.uk/sites/default/files/separation-divorce-factsheet-jan2014.pdf

ACKNOWLEDGEMENTS

My role as a dating coach on E4's flagship show *Celebs Go Dating*, running my private coaching practice, rushing around after my two young children, and making sure my husband gets a look-in every now and again mean life is very busy, albeit fulfilling. However, being a people person both professionally and personally, I have a natural love and affinity for helping people, which is why I really wanted to write this book on dating and relationships, something which resonates with so many of us.

When my fabulous publishers Bloomsbury got behind me again and trusted me to write another honest and heartfelt self-help guide, I couldn't have been more grateful. As I've learnt over the years, writing a book is a marathon not a sprint and I can't believe this is my fourth, so thank you to some very important people who helped this book *finally* unravel out of my head and onto a page.

Charlotte Croft – my editor extraordinaire, my wise owl, and one of the smartest and most beautiful (inside and out) women I know. Thank you for embarking on our third journey together. As always you take my work from a B- to an A+. I value you greatly.

Bloomsbury Publishing – I still pinch myself when I reflect on how I am part of your esteemed stable of authors. Thank you for your continued belief in me and for allowing me to keep writing books with you.

Samantha Mackenzie Weller – so much more than a manager – my friend, my sounding board, my confidante and all-round superwoman. Always going above and beyond, and it's always appreciated. You know how much you mean to me and I couldn't do any of this without you throwing up the tennis balls for me to whack into the net.

Team Belle PR – the most hard-working, talented ladies. I had the good fortune to meet you and continue to work alongside you. Thank you for giving your all and having my back always.

My folks, Peter and Mary – my relationship role models who have successfully weathered nearly fifty years as a married couple! Without your constant help with the kids and emergency rallying around, this book would, quite frankly, have been impossible to complete. My mother-in-law, Liz, ditto – we couldn't do without any of you!

And last but certainly not least, my darling husband Alex and my beautifully cheeky Vincenzo and Eleanora – this book is ultimately about love, and the love I have for you my little family is beyond words. You are my world. I do it all for you guys. A-Team per sempre.

ABOUT THE AUTHOR

Anna is an internationally revered and accredited Life Coach and Master NLP Practitioner. She is also the Dating Coach on E4's #1 rating show, Celebs Go Dating where alongside matchmaker Paul C. Brunson she helps celebrities find love.

She is a number one bestselling author, with her previous three books, Breaking Mad: The Insiders Guide to Conquering Anxiety, Breaking Mum and Dad: The Insiders Guide to Parenting Anxiety and How Not To Lose It: Mental Health Sorted available in multiple languages.

Anna is also a passionate ambassador for mental health and is very proud of her roles within Mind, Childline and The Prince's Trust.

Her proudest role though is being Mum to Vincenzo and Eleanora, and wife to husband Alex. They live in rural Hertfordshire.

INDEX